WILLOWS BY THE WATERCOURSES

Published by New Generation Publishing in 2022

First Edition

ISBN
      Paperback   978-1-80369-326-2
      Ebook   978-1-80369-327-9

www.newgeneration-publishing.com

New Generation Publishing

Introduction

The inspiration for this book title comes from the book of Isaiah. "For I will pour water on him who is thirsty, and floods on the dry ground; I will pour My Spirit on your descendants, and My blessing on your offspring; your offspring will spring up among the grass, like willows by the watercourses" (Isaiah 44:3–5 NKJV). "Willows" refers to a certain type of tree which will grow only near flowing water. Thus, "willows by the watercourses" paints a beautiful picture of well-being and flourishing. As a result of its strategic positioning and constant access to water, the willow thrives. Our Lord operates in our lives by His Word through His Spirit, both of which are referred to as "water" in Scripture. His desire for us is to be well watered, "like a well-watered garden, like a spring whose waters never fail" (Isaiah 58:11 NKJV). If you have holidayed in a hot climate, you may have noticed as you perambulated the streets that there was a remarkable difference between the gardens that had been faithfully irrigated and those that had been neglected and were dried up. God says, "I will pour water on him who is thirsty, and floods on the dry ground." He hydrates us as we imbibe the ever-flowing, overflowing streams of rejuvenation and refreshment found in His Word. It's my desire in writing this book that you are hydrated, flooded with light, that the grains of Truth garnered from His Word will take root deeply within, be refreshed by heavenly dew and harvested for His glory. May you experience copious streams of blessing in each devotional and become a channel of refreshment to others.

1

BOWL OF SLOP OR SLICE OF BEEF?

"The young lions suffer want and hunger; but those who seek the Lord lack no good thing."

Psalm 34:10 ESV

William Marion Runyan (1870–1957) penned the beautiful words: "Great is Thy faithfulness!"

Great is Thy faithfulness!
Morning by morning new mercies I see;
All I have needed Thy hand hath provided
Great is Thy faithfulness, Lord, unto me!

"All I have needed Thy hand hath provided." The Psalmist knew that firsthand, declaring in the well-known words, "The Lord is my shepherd, I lack nothing."[1] In a worry-laden culture, many see life through a lens of scarcity and lack. It's so refreshing to read the Psalms and note a mindset of provision and more than enough. In Psalm 34:10 David said, "The lions may grow weak and hungry, but those who seek the Lord lack no good thing."[2] Or, in the words of the Amplified Bible, "none of them shall lack any beneficial thing".[3] The motive continues, "No good thing will He withhold from those who walk uprightly."[4] Again, "You open Your hand and satisfy the desire of every living thing."[5]

---

[1] Psalm 23:1 NIV
[2] Psalm 34:10 NIV
[3] Psalm 34:10 AMPC
[4] Psalm 84:11 NKJV
[5] Psalm 145:16 NKJV

Our God is open-handed; He loves to give. He is the giver of every good and perfect gift – "Every good gift and every perfect gift is from above, and comes down from the Father of lights."[6] His storehouses never run empty. Do you need wisdom? He has a liberal supply for those who ask in faith. James tells us, "If any of you lacks wisdom, you should ask God, who gives generously"[7] Do you need grace? There is more than enough; in fact, abundant grace is available.

In a parable of Jesus recorded in Luke 15, the prodigal son was far from his father and it says, "he began to be in want".[8] We are told that when he came to himself, he said, "How many of my father's hired servants have bread enough and to spare, and I perish with hunger!"[9] The servants had bread enough and to spare. The Passion Translation reads, "There are many workers at my father's house who have all the food they want with plenty to spare. They lack nothing. Why am I here dying of hunger, feeding these pigs and eating their slop?" He returns to His Father, to the place of plenty, where he receives a robe, a ring and sandals (symbolic of sonship) and a slice of the fattened calf. His older brother is none too pleased, but note the words of the Father to him, "Son, you are always with me, and all that I have is yours."[10] All I have is yours. Allow those words to dissipate your worries and enter into the rest of faith in our God who is faithful.

---

[6] James 1:17 NIV
[7] James 1:5 NIV
[8] Luke 15:14 NKJV
[9] Luke 15:17 NJKV
[10] Luke 15:31 NKJV

2

COME FORTH AS GOLD

"But He knows the way that I take; when He has tested me, I shall come forth as gold."

Job 23:10 NKJV

In recent years the Western world has seen a surge in the upcycling of vintage and contemporary objects. Rather than dump a broken artefact in landfill, many items are salvaged and repurposed. Kintsugi is a centuries-old Japanese art form of fixing broken pottery. The name of the technique is derived from the words "Kin" (golden) and "tsugi" (joinery), which compound to mean "golden repair". Rather than rejoin ceramic pieces with a camouflaged adhesive, the artisan adopts the Kintsugi technique where a special lacquer with gold pigment is applied. Once completed, beautiful seams of gold glint in the conspicuous cracks of ceramic wares. Rather than disguise the scars and cracks, Kintsugi embraces authenticity and remembers each artefact's unique history. Often the character of the repaired piece is even more beautiful than the original, much stronger and revitalised.

Isn't it reassuring to know that we have a Potter? We are clay yielded to the hands of the Divine Potter who wants to shape us into a vessel of honour fit for His use. Hard times come and go as Job experienced, but he was able to testify, "I shall come forth as gold."[11] The apostle Paul had many trials in life. He endured beatings, stonings, imprisonment, hunger, cold, persecution, sleepless nights, shipwrecks and friends bailing out on him. Speaking of such he said, "You know that everyone in the province of Asia has deserted me." [12] That must have been gruelling. He had a thorn in his flesh which tormented him greatly. Three

---

[11] Job 23:10 NKJV
[12] 2 Timothy 1:15 NIV

times he pleaded with the Lord to take it away but the reply he got was, "My grace is sufficient for you, for my power is made perfect in weakness."[13] He went on to declare, "Therefore I will boast all the more gladly about my weaknesses, so that Christ's power may rest on me. That is why, for Christ's sake, I delight in weaknesses, in insults, in hardships, in persecutions, in difficulties. For when I am weak, then I am strong."[14]

Paul, like Job of old, emerged from his trials as pure gold. To the Roman believers he asserted, "And we know that in all things God works for the good of those who love him, who have been called according to his purpose."[15]

God works His liquid gold into the crevices and pours grace into the cracks of your life bringing forth redemptive beauty. You are His workmanship. He is actively working in you. He is the Perfecter of your faith. He is putting the finishing touches to your life as Philippians 1:6 says, "I pray with great faith for you, because I'm fully convinced that the One who began this glorious work in you will faithfully continue the process of maturing you and will put his finishing touches to it until the unveiling of our Lord Jesus Christ!"[16]

---

[13] 2 Corinthians 12:9 NIV
[14] 2 Corinthians 12:9–10 NIV
[15] Romans 8:28 NIV
[16] Philippians 1:6 TPT

3

NEWTON'S CRADLE

*"A new commandment I give to you, that you love one another; as
I have loved you, that you also love one another."*

.   *John 13:34 NKJV*

*I*nstead of conventional ornaments such as Royal Doulton, Wedgewood, Waterford Crystal or Belleek, our home has some rather unusual enhancements. One such "ornament" is an ingenious device known as Newton's Cradle. Using a series of suspended metal spheres it demonstrates the conservation of momentum. When a ball on one end of the cradle is lifted and released, it strikes the stationary spheres. This collision creates a force which causes the ball on the opposite end to swing in the opposite direction. It is named after the English scientist Sir Isaac Newton and it aptly illustrates his three laws of motion. The first law states that a body remains at rest unless acted upon by an outside force. The second law states that the force of an object is equal to its mass times its acceleration. Newton's Third Law of Motion, perhaps the most famous, says that "for every action, there is an equal and opposite reaction." This is true in our everyday lives. When you smile at someone, the person smiles back. A yawn when witnessed by another usually results in a yawn. Or, in a toxic, divisive, flammable environment, a sarcastic comment can produce a sarcastic comment back.

Our actions and reactions matter immensely. We are to be kingdom responders who, knowing that we are so loved, love in return. We love because He first loved us. God moved in love and demonstrated His own love for us, even when we were unlovely. As His followers Jesus says to us, "A new commandment I give to you, that you love one another; as I have loved you, that you also love one another."[17] Or, as John the

---

[17] John 13:34 NKJV

beloved disciple phrased it, "Beloved children, our love can't be an abstract theory we only talk about, but a way of life demonstrated through our loving deeds";[18] "Those who are loved by God, let his love continually pour from you to one another, because God is love";[19] and, "Delightfully loved ones, if he loved us with such tremendous love, then 'loving one another should be our way of life!'"[20]

When we show love to others, we are really loving Jesus. He said, "And the King will answer them, 'Don't you know? When you cared for one of the least important of these my little ones, my true brothers and sisters, you demonstrated love for me.'"[21] On the other hand, Paul, formerly known as Saul, tells us explicitly that before becoming a follower of Jesus he was a persecutor of the people of God. He led a violent persecution of the young Christian church in Jerusalem, going from house to house, dragging men and women off to prison. Acts 9 tells of his conversion experience, "As he neared Damascus on his journey, suddenly a light from heaven flashed around him. He fell to the ground and heard a voice say to him 'Saul, Saul, why do you persecute me? ... I am Jesus, whom you are persecuting.'"[22] Instead of "Why do you persecute My Church?" Jesus says, "Why do you persecute Me?" In persecuting the followers of Jesus, Saul was persecuting Jesus too.

As recipients of such immense love, let us demonstrate that same love to others. Let us show "the more excellent way".

---

[18] 1 John 3:18 TPT
[19] 1 John 4:7 TPT
[20] 1 John 4:11 TPT
[21] Matthew 25:40 TPT
[22] Acts 9:3–5 NIV

4

ALLOW SUBSTITUTIONS

"He gives power to the weak, and to those who have no might He increases strength. Even the youths shall faint and be weary, and the young men shall utterly fall, but those who wait on the Lord shall renew their strength; they shall mount up with wings like eagles, they shall run and not be weary, they shall walk and not faint."

Isaiah 40:29–31 NKJV

Being able to shop online is so convenient, isn't it? Earlier this year I ventured into the experience of shopping virtually for groceries. Having booked my preferred window of time for delivery, I started popping the staples into a virtual basket and quickly crossed the threshold of spending in order to get free delivery. Then, having succumbed to the marketing technique "suggested for you", I soon incorporated edibles surplus to requirements. I also opted for "allow substitutions". The idea is that when a product in your order is not available, a substitute item is offered. Sounds good but no system is perfect, which resulted in some unusual and unusable substitutions, one such being a glass bottle of green olives instead of Olivio oil for frying. I guess it was still "a touch of the Mediterranean". I have since heard of others receiving toilet roll instead of cat litter; a bunch of roses instead of chocolate Roses; and a fresh fruit salad substituted with peach-scented shampoo.

Isaiah 40:31 speaks of renewing strength. The Hebrew word for "renew" is "chalaph" meaning "to substitute, alter, change for better". When the Lord substitutes something, it is always for the better and for our good. He gives strength in place of weariness and weakness, fresh strength instead of exhaustion. Are you ready for this kind of revitalisation? The prerequisite is that we wait on the Lord. Paul declared in Philippians 4:13, "I can do all things through Christ who strengthens me."[23] He strengthens us, in Greek "endunamao" which is a compound of "en" and "dunamis". The word "en" means "into", and "dunamis" means power, ability, force, might. When combined it means to infuse with supernatural strength. In the Old Testament Septuagint "dunamis" was primarily used to picture the combined forces of an entire fighting army! It is wise to "allow substitutions" and let God renew our strength.

In Isaiah 61:3 we see His further amazing substitutions – "to give them beauty for ashes, the oil of joy for mourning, the garment of praise for the spirit of heaviness".[24] In exchange for ashes we receive beauty; in exchange for mourning, the oil of joy; and in exchange for the spirit of heaviness we receive the garment of praise. How great is our God! Let us put on that mantle of joyous praise. Let us receive the oil of joy and diadem of beauty. Let us accept the fresh strength available for today. Allow these substitutions? Yes, please!

---

[23] Philippians 4:13 NKJV
[24] Isaiah 61:3 NKJV

5

X MARKS THE SPOT

"For our spiritual wealth is in him, like hidden treasure waiting to be discovered – heaven's wisdom and endless riches of revelation knowledge."

Colossians 2:3 TPT

The enigmatic letter x represents many things and has many diverse uses. For example, the "x factor" refers to a noteworthy quality or talent. The letter "x" is often used in algebra to mean a value that is not yet known. It is called a variable, e.g., $x + 2 = 7$. In basic maths, $\times$ is the symbol for multiplication: $8 \times 8 = 64$. It can also appear on your assignment after the calculation to signify an error. In organic chemistry x stands for any halogen group. In physics the variable x is often used to represent the horizontal position. It is also used between figures indicating dimensions such as a photo frame: $4'' \times 6''$ (read as "four by six inches"). On a card x symbolises a kiss. It defines a generation, Generation X. On clothing it expresses size, X for large, XL for extra large. As a Roman numeral x represents ten. A person unable to write their name may put x in place of a signature. On ballot papers x indicates the choice of candidate. The letter x shortens Christmas to xmas, the initial Greek letter in the word Christ, Χριστός. Robert Louis Stevenson in *Treasure Island* made x popular – x marks the spot of hidden treasure.

X marks the spot. Buried treasure is one of those things that sounds like it only exists in adventure novels. However, throughout history valuable coins, jewellery and other artefacts have often been either deliberately buried or lost to the ages. In God's Word we find a treasure trove awaiting our discovery, treasures which God has hidden for his lovers. The Psalmist testifies, "Your word I have treasured in my heart".[25] "Everything you speak to me is like joyous treasure, filling my life with gladness."[26] "I rejoice at Your word as one who finds great treasure."[27] "Your promises are the source of my bubbling joy; the revelation of your word thrills me like one who has discovered hidden treasure."[28] "The rarest treasures of life are found in His truth. That's why I prize God's Word like others prize the finest gold. Nothing brings the soul such sweetness as seeking his living words."[29]

It all testifies to Jesus, the One of whom Paul wrote, "Living within you is the Christ who floods you with the expectation of glory! This mystery of Christ, embedded within us, becomes a heavenly treasure chest of hope filled with the riches of glory for his people, and God wants everyone to know it!"[30] and "For our spiritual wealth is in him, like hidden treasure waiting to be discovered – heaven's wisdom and endless riches of revelation knowledge."[31] Is your daily life an adventure of discovery? Great treasure awaits.

---

[25] Psalm 119:11 NASB
[26] Psalm 119:111 TPT
[27] Psalm 119:162 NLT
[28] Psalm 119:162 TPT
[29] Psalm 19:10 TPT
[30] Colossians 1:27 TPT
[31] Colossians 2:3 TPT

6

ENVELOPED ... DEVELOPED

"Consider it pure joy, my brothers and sisters, whenever you face trials of many kinds, because you know that the testing of your faith produces perseverance. Let perseverance finish its work so that you may be mature and complete, not lacking anything."

James 1:2–4 NIV

Historians believe that the ubiquitous item of stationery which we call the envelope made its first appearance in ancient China, where its purpose was to guarantee the privacy of royal correspondence. However, unlike the version we have today, it was made from clay and moulded into a hollow sphere, in which the message was placed. It was sealed with more wet clay, then baked, causing it to harden and ensuring the tablet's contents were safe inside. It was smashed to reveal the contents upon delivery.

By the second century BC, paper envelopes were developed, and used in China to enclose monetary gifts. It wasn't until the medieval era that production techniques improved to such an extent that a paper envelope could be used for sending messages. Even then, however, the design was little more than an extra sheet of paper folded over the message and sealed with wax. The Industrial Revolution changed the envelope forever with the first envelope-making machine. Later would emerge the pre-gum envelope and the window envelope. The word "envelope" comes from the French "envelopper" (to envelop).

James 1:2–4 reminds us that when we are enveloped in trials, we have an opportunity to become developed in character. "Consider it wholly joyful, my brethren, whenever you are enveloped in or encounter trials of any sort or fall into various temptations. Be assured and understand that the trial and proving of your faith bring out endurance and steadfastness and patience. But let endurance and steadfastness and patience have full play and do a thorough work, so that you may be [people] perfectly and fully developed [with no defects], lacking in nothing."[32]

Another translation reads, "My fellow believers, when it seems as though you are facing nothing but difficulties see it as an invaluable opportunity to experience the greatest joy that you can! For you know that when your faith is tested it stirs up power within you to endure all things. And then as your endurance grows even stronger it will release perfection into every part of your being until there is nothing missing and nothing lacking."[33]

See it as an invaluable opportunity! The Message translation says, "You know that under pressure, your faith-life is forced into the open and shows its true colors. So don't try to get out of anything prematurely. Let it do its work so you become mature and well-developed, not deficient in any way."[34]

When James writes, "whenever you face trials of many kinds",[35] the word for "many kinds" is "poikilos" meaning various kinds, manifold, variegated (like the autumn leaves). Our trials may be many-coloured, but so is the grace of God; 1 Peter 4:10 uses the same word "poikilos" of the manifold grace of God. For the manifold trials in which you are enveloped, there is manifold grace available. His grace is sufficient for every situation.

---

[32] James 1:2–4 AMPC
[33] James 1:2–4 TPT
[34] James 1:2–4 MSG
[35] James 1:2–4 MSG

7

MY HELPER

"For He Himself has said, 'I will never leave you nor forsake you.'
So we may boldly say: 'The Lord is my helper; I will not fear. What
can man do to me?'"

Hebrews 13:5–6 NKJV

"The Lord is my helper."[36] Actually there is no verb "is" in the Greek here, so it reads, "The Lord my helper!" Let's zoom in on the word "helper", in Greek, "boethos". This is an intriguing noun from the verb "beoetheo", a compound of "boe", meaning "a cry" and "theo" meaning "to run". Thus "beoetheo" gives the reassuring picture of one who runs on hearing a cry, to give assistance or meet an urgent distress call. In Homeric Greek it was used in a military sense for responding to a war-cry. In Acts 27:17 Luke supplements our understanding of this word in his use of the related noun form, "boetheia".

In context this chapter is the account of Paul's shipwreck on Malta during his journey to Rome. The ship had sustained a substantial amount of damage because of the buffeting of relentless gales. The crew had much-needed repair work to do before they could continue on their journey. Verse 17 describes their actions, "They used supports to undergird the ship".[37] Here "supports" is the word "boetheia". It refers specifically to a rope or chain for frapping a vessel to keep the beams from separating and to brace the hull, which was in danger of breaking apart under the strain of the storm.

This background should enable us to grasp the meaning behind our word boethos, helper. The Lord is my helper. He has said, "I will never leave you nor forsake you."[38] Literally, I will not loosen my hold of you

---

[36] Hebrews 13:6 NKJV
[37] Acts 27:17 ESV
[38] Hebrews 13:5–6 NKJV

or fail to uphold you. I will not let you sink. I will not leave you in dire straits. As the Amplified Bible phrases verse 5, "He [God] Himself has said, 'I will not in any way fail you nor give you up nor leave you without support. [I will] not, [I will] not, [I will] not in any degree leave you helpless nor forsake nor let [you] down (relax My hold on you)! [Assuredly not!]'".[39]

Because of what God has said, we can boldly say "The Lord is my helper; I will not fear. What can man do to me?" The writer of Hebrews is looking back to Psalm 118:6, "The Lord is on my side; I will not fear. What can man do to me?"[40] He is on your side. He runs to your aid. He furnishes you with the help you need. His Word tells us in Hebrews 4:16, "So let us come boldly to the throne of our gracious God. There we will receive his mercy, and we will find grace to help us when we need it most."[41] The Amplified version describes this "help" (boetheia) as "appropriate help and well-timed help, coming just when we need it".[42] Let Him undergird you with His strong, loving arms and make it possible for your vessel to get through the storms of life without succumbing to the circumstances. Be confident that He is on your side. He is your Helper.

---

[39] Hebrews 13:5–6 AMPC
[40] Psalm 118:6 NKJV
[41] Hebrews 4:16 NLT
[42] Hebrews 4:16 AMPC

8

CROWNED

"who beautifies, dignifies, and crowns you with loving-kindness and tender mercy."

Psalm 103:4 AMPC

rowns. They're an uncommon commodity in our culture, worn only by monarchs and royalty. If I asked you, "Do you have a crown?" you may answer in the affirmative only if you have visited the dentist and acquired an artificial covering for your compromised or broken tooth. In that case I have a few. Or maybe you are a numismatist and can show me your collection of old British crowns minted many years ago, each worth five shillings or 25 pence. In that sense, I have one crown. Or perhaps you are a draughts player and have promoted a piece to king by placing another on top of it, thus acquiring a crown.

Today's verse mentions God crowning us. I have always appreciated the benefits of God listed in Psalm 103 – He forgives. He heals. He redeems. He crowns. He satisfies. He renews. "Bless the Lord, O my soul; and all that is within me, bless His holy name! Bless the Lord, O my soul, and forget not all His benefits: who forgives all your iniquities, who heals all your diseases, who redeems your life from destruction, who crowns you with loving-kindness and tender mercies, who satisfies your mouth with good things, so that your youth is renewed like the eagle's."[43]

Notice in particular the words, "He crowns us with loving-kindness and tender mercies."[44] Pause and think of that. You are crowned with loving-kindness and tender mercies. The Amplified Bible reads, "who beautifies, dignifies, and crowns you with loving-kindness and tender

---

[43] Psalm 103:1–5 NKJV
[44] Psalm 103:4 NKJV

mercy".[45] The Hebrew word for "loving-kindness" is "hesed", meaning "the steadfast covenantal love of God".

To discover how much the Psalmist valued this loving-kindness, read Psalm 136 where it is mentioned in every one of the twenty-six verses. I love how this word (hesed) is translated in *The Jesus Storybook Bible*, "Never-Stopping, Never-Giving-Up, Unbreaking, Always and Forever Love."

You are crowned with hesed. You are also crowned with tender mercies, "racham" in Hebrew. Those same two words, hesed and racham, appear in Lamentations 3:22, "The faithful love of the Lord (hesed) never ends! His mercies (racham) never cease. Great is his faithfulness; his mercies begin afresh each morning."[46]

These words distinguish and define us as the people of God. Furthermore, the Bible says, "Blessings crown the head of the righteous";[47] "For the Lord delights in his people; he crowns the humble with victory";[48] and "to bestow on them a crown of beauty instead of ashes". [49] Treasure the multiplied blessings and eternal benefits bestowed on us. We have a crown that covers us in unconditional love and overwhelming compassion. Remember to allow that same love and compassion to flow to others that they may come to know Him too. You are crowned for the Lord's renown.

---

[45] Psalm 103:4 AMPC
[46] Lamentations 3:22–23 NLT (words in brackets mine)
[47] Proverbs 10:6 NIV
[48] Psalm 149:4 NIV
[49] Isaiah 61:3 NIV

9

WAITING IN THE WINGS

"But for you who fear my name, the Sun of Righteousness will rise with healing in his wings"

Malachi 4:2 NLT

aiting in the wings" is an idiom with an interesting origin. The idiom is derived from the world of theatre. The wings of a theatre are the areas on each side of the stage where actors wait before they make an appearance. It is where they observe the activity on the stage without being seen by the audience. They wait in the wings before it is their time to go on the stage. Understudy actors often wait in the wings watching the performance in anticipation of taking over a role from the main actor. In addition, someone holding a script waits in the wings, a helpful aid for forgetful and unprepared actors. Another expression, "to wing it" comes from this action.

Today I want to ask you a question – Are you waiting in the wings of God? The wings of God are a tremendous place of security for the believer. In Ruth 2:12, Boaz encourages the young Moabite widow Ruth with these words: "May the Lord, the God of Israel, under whose wings you have come to take refuge, reward you fully for what you have done."[50] David writes, "Keep me as the apple of your eye; hide me in the shadow of your wings."[51] Again, "How precious is Your steadfast love, O God! The children of men take refuge and put their trust under the shadow of Your wings."[52] "Be merciful to me, O God, be merciful to me! For my soul trusts in You; and in the shadow of Your wings I

---

[50] Ruth 2:12 NLT
[51] Psalm 17:8 ESV
[52] Psalm 36:7 AMPC

will make my refuge".[53] The beautiful words of Psalm 91 remind us, "He will cover you with his pinions, and under his wings you will find refuge; his faithfulness is a shield and buckler."[54]

The wings of God are a magnificent place of intimacy. Exodus 25:20,22 tells us, "And the cherubim shall spread out their wings above, covering the mercy seat with their wings, facing each other and looking down toward the mercy seat …There I will meet with you and, from above the mercy seat, from between the two cherubim that are upon the ark of the Testimony, I will speak intimately with you of all which I will give you in commandment to the Israelites."[55]

The wings of God are an amazing place of healing. "But for you who fear my name, the Sun of Righteousness will rise with healing in his wings. And you will go free, leaping with joy like calves let out to pasture."[56] This prophecy of the Messiah from Malachi was beautifully demonstrated when the woman who had the issue of blood touched the "border of his garment". The garment was known as the "Tallit", the corners of which were referred to as "wings". Luke states, "Now a woman, having a flow of blood for twelve years, who had spent all her livelihood on physicians and could not be healed by any, came from behind and touched the border of His garment. And immediately her flow of blood stopped."[57] This woman touched the "border of his garment". It is believed that she touched the "wings" of His Tallit, in faith that He was the Messiah as spoken of by the prophet Malachi, and would thus have "healing in his wings".

Are you waiting in the wings – the place of security, intimacy and healing?

---

[53] Psalm 57:1 NKJV
[54] Psalm 57:1 NKJV
[55] Exodus 25:20,22 AMPC
[56] Malachi 4:2 NLT
[57] Luke 8:43–44 NKJV

10

I HEARD … I TURNED … I SAW … I FELL

"When I saw him, I fell at his feet as if I were dead. But he laid his right hand on me and said, 'Don't be afraid! I am the First and the Last.'."

Revelation 1:17 NLT

*J*ohn witnessed the mighty miracles and ministry of Jesus first-hand. He related amazing accounts in his book, but he also said, "And truly Jesus did many other signs in the presence of His disciples, which are not written in this book."[58] In fact we are told, "And there are also many other things that Jesus did, which if they were written one by one, I suppose that even the world itself could not contain the books that would be written."[59]

John was privileged to be part of the inner circle. Along with Peter and James, John got to witness Jesus do things no one else saw. He witnessed the transfiguration and became an eyewitness of His majesty. Jesus was transfigured before them. His face shone like the sun, and His clothes became as white as the light. On the night of His betrayal, in the Garden of Gethsemane, Jesus took Peter, James and John with Him to pray, and asked them to keep watch. John had the distinction of being known as the beloved disciple who intimately communed with the Lord. He witnessed the cross and was entrusted with the care of Jesus' mother. He witnessed the empty tomb where "he saw and believed".[60] For forty days he witnessed the "many infallible proofs"[61] of the Risen Lord. But nothing prepared John for when he was bodily on the isle of Patmos but spiritually caught up in the Spirit and revealed the consummation of the

---

[58] John 20:30 NKJV
[59] John 21:25 NKJV
[60] John 20:8 NKJV
[61] Acts 1:3 NKJV

ages. He heard behind him a loud voice, as of a trumpet, saying, "I am the Alpha and the Omega, the First and the Last."[62] As he turned to see the voice that spoke to him, he was overwhelmed. "And when I saw Him, I fell at His feet as dead. But He laid His right hand on me, saying to me, 'Do not be afraid; I am the First and the Last.'."[63] He was overcome by the vision of the glorified Christ.

What John saw human words can only approximate. John recorded a description of Christ's appearance, apparel and authority. "And having turned I saw seven golden lampstands, and in the midst of the seven lampstands One like the Son of Man, clothed with a garment down to the feet and girded about the chest with a golden band. His head and hair were white like wool, as white as snow, and His eyes like a flame of fire; His feet were like fine brass, as if refined in a furnace, and His voice as the sound of many waters; He had in His right hand seven stars, out of His mouth went a sharp two-edged sword, and His countenance was like the sun shining in its strength."[64]

Jesus is revealed in all of His glory and splendour. Can I encourage you to allow this portrait of Jesus to strengthen your relationship with Him? Today's church needs a fresh glimpse of the glorified Christ. John writes, "I heard … I turned … I saw… I fell …" Hear that voice – so regal. Turn and see the Altogether Lovely One – so resplendent. Then fall at His feet in awe of Him.

---

[62] Revelation 1:11 NKJV
[63] Revelation 1:17 NKJV
[64] Revelation 1:12–16 NKJV

11

BE RESOLUTE

"Keep your eyes open, hold tight to your convictions, give it all you've got, be resolute, and love without stopping."

1 Corinthians 16:13 MSG

heck out the meaning of the word "resolution" in a dictionary:

A firm decision to do or not to do something.
The quality of being determined or resolute.
The capability of a microscope, or other optical instrument, to show things clearly and with a lot of detail.
The act of separating or being separated into clearly constituent parts, such as the resolution of oil into bitumen and tar.
A formal decision taken at a meeting by means of a vote.

The word is employed in diverse ways and shares the same Latin root as "resolute" and "resolve". We see a resolute Jesus in Luke 9:51, "As the time approached for him to be taken up to heaven, Jesus resolutely set out for Jerusalem."[65] Another translation states, "so strong with resolve, Jesus made Jerusalem His destination".[66] Another reads, "He steadfastly and determinedly set His face to go to Jerusalem."[67]

Jesus was fully aware that suffering and death on a cross awaited Him. He knew He had to die in our place to pay for our sins. And He was determined to accomplish His mission.

Paul chose to wrap up his words to the Corinthians with a brief statement designed to grab their attention. He tells them, and us, "Keep

---

[65] Luke 9:51 NIV
[66] Luke 9:51 The Voice
[67] Luke 9:51 AMPC

your eyes open, hold tight to your convictions, give it all you've got, be resolute, and love without stopping." [68] His words are loaded with intention, purpose and conviction to help the reader take on life with full-throttle determination. What would life look like if we all took this onboard and kept our eyes open, held tight to our convictions, gave it all we've got? What if each of us were resolute and loved without stopping?

Many people and situations can try to break our resolve as in the case of the building of the Temple recorded in the Book of Ezra. The peoples around them set out to discourage their effort. Ezra 4:4–5 states, "So these people started beating down the morale of the people of Judah, harassing them as they built. They even hired propagandists to sap their resolve. They kept this up for about fifteen years, throughout the lifetime of Cyrus king of Persia and on into the reign of Darius king of Persia." [69]

Who or what is trying to sap your resolve? Again, remind yourself, "Keep your eyes open, hold tight to your convictions, give it all you've got, be resolute, and love without stopping." Read the biographies of the people you admire and, almost without exception, you will find these threads woven into their life-fabric. They were unwavering, uncompromising, unshakable, courageous, relentless and strong! They were resolute. I ponder Jonathan Edwards' resolutions: "Resolution One: I will live for God. Resolution Two: If no one else does, I still will." [70] Are you resolute to live for God no matter what the cost?

---

[68] 1 Corinthians 16:13 MSG
[69] Ezra 4:4–5 MSG
[70] goodreads.com/quotes/593647

12

LACKLUSTRE

"For once you were darkness, but now you are light in the Lord; walk as children of Light [lead the lives of those native-born to the Light]."

Ephesians 5:8 AMPC

No English curriculum is complete without a mandatory measure of William Shakespeare.

The Bard of Avon and his works are titans of linguistic and literary history. He was a prolific inventor of words, some lost in the mists of time, others still in common usage today. For example, "unfriending" someone predates the sphere of social media. The word "unfriended" appears in the works of *Twelfth Night* and *King Lear*. "Green-eyed" (jealous) emerged in *The Merchant of Venice*. Shakespeare gave the first recorded instance of the phrase "one fell swoop" in *Macbeth*. The word "hazel" is first recorded as a word describing the colour of eyes in *Romeo and Juliet*. The word "lacklustre" first entered circulation in *As You Like It*. It's a combination of the Germanic "lack" and "lustre", meaning "shine", from the Latin "lustrare", or "to brighten".

"Lacklustre" means "lacking force, brilliance, or vitality". [71] Suggested synonyms are: boring, dull, flat, uninspired, dim, leaden, matt, unilluminated. There is nothing dull or lacklustre about God. In fact, light is one of the most prevalent themes throughout the entire Bible. God is the "Father of lights";[72] we are "children of light".[73] Paul

---

[71] dictionary.com
[72] James 1:17 NKJV
[73] Ephesians 5:8 NKJV

wrote, "You are all children of the light and children of the day. We do not belong to the night or to the darkness."[74]

The opposite of lacklustre is bright, enthusiastic, lively, shining. As children of light, we are to walk in the light. In fact, Proverbs 4:18 states, "But the lovers of God walk on the highway of light, and their way shines brighter and brighter until they bring forth the perfect day."[75] Jesus told us, "You are the light of the world. A city that is set on a hill cannot be hidden. Nor do they light a lamp and put it under a basket, but on a lampstand, and it gives light to all who are in the house. Let your light so shine before men, that they may see your good works and glorify your Father in heaven."[76]

Have you noticed how light quality is affected by pollution? We have a candleholder centralised on the kitchen table, with a glass shade encasing the candle and flame. We light the candle when we are all present for an evening meal, but I have noticed that over time the glass becomes blackened and dull with carbon residue, and rather than it reflecting the light, the flame can barely be seen. The light was the same, but the vessel containing it had fallen prey to pollution. Are we reflecting the Light, or has our light dimmed? Has sin dulled the evidence of Christ in you? Let nothing dim the light that shines from within. Shine brightly! As Paul stated, "You are to live clean, innocent lives as children of God in a dark world full of people who are crooked and stubborn. Shine out among them like beacon lights, holding out to them the Word of Life."[77]

We are the beacon lights who speak Life! The Greek word for beacon light is "phoster" – an illuminator with brilliancy. It is the root of the word "phosphorus" which is a light-bearing substance that glows in the dark. May we not lack lustre but may our lumen output be effective as we shine with the inner incandescent light of God.

---

74 1 Thessalonians 5:5 NIV
75 Proverbs 4:18 TPT
76 Matthew 5:14–16 NKJV
77 Philippians 2:15–16 LB

13

DISORIENTED

"You're blessed when you stay on course, walking steadily on the road revealed by God. You're blessed when you follow his directions, doing your best to find him."

Psalm 119:1–2 MSG

The word "disoriented" means "to cause to lose one's bearings". If you check the etymology of the word, it specifically means that you do not know in which direction the sun will rise – that is, which way is east. The base word comes from the Latin "orientem", which means "the east". To orient yourself is to know which way the sun will rise, and an orientation helps you point yourself in the right direction. If you have been involved in orienteering, you will know that the objective is to follow a pre-set trail. It involves navigating, against the clock, on a long unfamiliar trail, checking in at various points along the way. You need a map and compass to compete, and a lot of stamina and the ability to stay the course. The map reveals to you the terrain in which you are moving, while the compass gives you a constant point of reference.

The Psalmist declared, "You're blessed when you stay on course, walking steadily on the road revealed by God. You're blessed when you follow his directions, doing your best to find him."[78] It is important that we stay on course and stay the course.

He went on to say, "That's right – you don't go off on your own; you walk straight along the road he set."[79] He prayed, "Oh, that my steps might be steady, keeping to the course you set."[80] He declared, "I'm

---

[78] Psalm 119:1–2 MSG
[79] Psalm 119:3 MSG
[80] Psalm 119:5 MSG

single-minded in pursuit of you; don't let me miss the road signs you've posted."[81]

The Bible tells us that the double-minded man is unstable in all his ways and will not receive what he asks of God (James 1:7–8). Thus, single-mindedness is a worthy pursuit. The Psalmist pleaded, "Barricade the road that goes Nowhere; grace me with your clear revelation."[82] He affirmed, "I'll run the course you lay out for me if you'll just show me how"[83] and "I watch for your ancient landmark words, and know I'm on the right track."[84]

The terrain may change, the pace may vary, but the course is set for each one of us to run. He's given us the roadmap of His Word to help us navigate, and the Holy Spirit to help us follow. He gives us our point of reference: "And let us run with endurance the race God has set before us. We do this by keeping our eyes on Jesus, the champion who initiates and perfects our faith."[85] If you're off course right now or disoriented, go back to the Bible and seek the leading of the Holy Spirit. You can get back on course and finish your race well.

---

[81] Psalm 119: 10 MSG
[82] Psalm 119: 29 MSG
[83] Psalm 119:32 MSG
[84] Psalm 119:52 MSG
[85] Hebrews 12:1–2 NLT

14

WE HAD HOPED

"And beginning at Moses and all the Prophets, He expounded to them in all the Scriptures the things concerning Himself."
Luke 24:27 NKJV

The events on the road to Emmaus are discussed in Luke 24. This is the longest single post-resurrection account in the gospels. As two disciples trudged from Jerusalem to Emmaus (seven miles), Jesus joined them. The disciples related their shattered hopes and dreams. Their idea of redemption had been decimated by the death of Jesus. In their own words they aptly relayed their despondency, "We had hoped that he was the one who was going to redeem Israel."[86]

"We had hoped." So many are living with dashed hopes at the moment. But there is a beautiful carol which speaks of "a thrill of hope".

O holy night! The stars are brightly shining,
It is the night of our dear Saviour's birth.
Long lay the world in sin and error pining,
Till He appear'd and the soul felt its worth.
A thrill of hope, the weary world rejoices,
For yonder breaks a new and glorious morn.[87]

Where have you set your hope? The Psalmist said, "Why, my soul, are you downcast? Why so disturbed within me? Put your hope in God, for I will yet praise him, my Savior and my God."[88] God has plans to give

---

[86] Luke 24:21 NIV
[87] "O Holy Night", translated from French to English by John Sullivan Dwight, Esq., c. 1858 (1813–1893).
[88] Psalm 42:5 NIV

you hope and a future. [89] When Paul thought of the Thessalonian believers, this is what came to mind, "We remember before our God and Father your work produced by faith, your labor prompted by love, and your endurance inspired by hope in our Lord Jesus Christ."[90] Is your endurance inspired by hope in the Lord Jesus? We have "a living hope through the resurrection of Jesus Christ from the dead".[91] My prayer for you is Romans 15:13, "May the God of hope fill you with all joy and peace as you trust in him, so that you may overflow with hope by the power of the Holy Spirit."[92] Or, as another translation beautifully phrases it, "Now may God, the inspiration and fountain of hope, fill you to overflowing with uncontainable joy and perfect peace as you trust in him. And may the power of the Holy Spirit continually surround your life with his super-abundance until you radiate with hope!"[93] I pray too that you are "prepared to give an answer to everyone who asks you to give the reason for the hope that you have".[94]

May we see the weary world rejoice! And remember, "Let us hold unswervingly to the hope we profess, for he who promised is faithful."[95]

---

[89] Jeremiah 29:11 NIV
[90] 1 Thessalonians 1:3 NIV
[91] 1 Peter 1:3 NIV
[92] Romans 15:13 NIV
[93] Romans 15:13 TPT
[94] 1 Peter 3:15 NIV
[95] Hebrews 10:23 NIV

15

140 MINUTES WELL SPENT

"And beginning at Moses and all the Prophets, He expounded to them in all the Scriptures the things concerning Himself."

Luke 24:27 NKJV

Continuing on the road to Emmaus, we find the words of Jesus, "Then He said to them, 'O foolish ones, and slow of heart to believe in all that the prophets have spoken! Ought not the Christ to have suffered these things and to enter into His glory?' And beginning at Moses and all the Prophets, He expounded to them in all the Scriptures the things concerning Himself."[96]

He expounded to them in all the Scriptures the things concerning Himself. This is such a powerful sentence. To two confounded disciples, He expounded to them what they needed to know concerning Himself. Let us catch the meaning of the Greek word translated as "expounded". It is "diermeneuo", a compound of "hermeneuo", which means "to interpret" and "dia" which means "fully" or "thoroughly". Thus, when compounded it means to unfold the meaning of what is said, to explain thoroughly, to translate into one's native language. For example, the same word is used in Acts 9:36, "At Joppa there was a certain disciple named Tabitha, which is translated Dorcas." Jesus made the meaning clear and showed how the Old Testament spoke of Him. Would you not have loved to have been a part of that small-group Bible study? The living Word expounding the written Word! He expounded "in all the Scriptures" the things concerning Himself. Earlier in the Gospels Jesus stated, "You study the Scriptures diligently because you think that in them you have eternal life. These are the very Scriptures that testify

---

96 Luke 24:25–27 NKJV

about me."[97] In other words, the entire message of the Bible is one finger pointing to the Lord Jesus Christ. It is testifying about Christ.

The road to Emmaus, verse 13 tells us, was seven miles. That's slightly over eleven kilometres. The average walking speed of a human is three to four miles per hour, or a mile every fifteen to twenty minutes. The total walk would have been around one hundred and forty minutes, more than two hours. What did Jesus cover? Did He mention the ram caught in the thicket offered up by Abraham in Genesis 22, a foreshadowing of the suffering of the Lord Jesus Christ, a substitutionary suffering? Did He refer to the Passover lamb which must be slain, and the blood applied to the lintels of the door? He could have worked through the entire Levitical sacrificial system, all a foreshadowing of the sufferings of the Lord Jesus Christ. Perhaps He turned to Isaiah 53 which speaks of how He must suffer. He must be pierced for our transgressions. He must be crushed for our iniquities. He must suffer our chastening and our scourging. He must be oppressed. He must be afflicted. He must be cut off from the land of the living. We are simply told He expounded "in all the Scriptures" what testified to Him.

Just before Jesus disappeared from the two on that road, Luke 24:31– 32 relates what happened next: "And their eyes were opened, and they knew him; and he vanished out of their sight. And they said one to another, 'Did not our heart burn within us, while he talked with us by the way, and while he opened to us the scriptures?'"[98]

Notice that their hearts burned as Jesus spoke to them and opened the Scriptures to them. I encourage you – talk to Jesus along the way. Let Him open the Scriptures to you. A Christ encounter can change everything.

---

[97] John 5:39 NIV
[98] Luke 24:31–32 KJV

16

LESSONS FROM HIS LINEAGE

"That at that time ye were without Christ, being aliens from the commonwealth of Israel, and strangers from the covenants of promise, having no hope, and without God in the world: But now in Christ Jesus ye who sometimes were far off are made nigh by the blood of Christ."

Ephesians 2:12–13 KJV

The opening sentence in a book should grip us and encourage us to read on. With that in mind, who would choose to open their book with a genealogy? Matthew did. He opened his gospel with a list of forty-two names. Before he presented the wise men, he stated that, "Abraham begot Isaac, Isaac begot Jacob, and Jacob begot Judah and his brothers. Judah begot Perez and Zerah by Tamar, Perez begot Hezron, and Hezron begot Ram."[99] Most Christians don't get overexcited about genealogies and typically skim over them. However, every word is given for good purpose. What can we learn from the lineage of Jesus?

We see that God is sovereign over history and working His purposes out. We can trust that His purposes are being fulfilled. Romans 8:28 says, "And we know that all things work together for good to those who love God, to those who are the called according to His purpose."[100]

We also learn that God knows your name. If you feel overlooked, insignificant, or that there is nothing special about you, remember this, God knows your name. He calls His own sheep by name. He cares for you. You are on a first-name basis with God.

From the genealogy we see that we are part of something much bigger, something that spans centuries. It is helpful to remember that

---

[99] Matthew 1:2–4 NKJV
[100] Romans 8:28 NKJV

there are great multitudes of believers who have gone before us, have faced the same struggles that we face, have called upon the Lord and walked by faith. The writer of Hebrews mentions this in chapter 11 where he lists faithful men and women who have gone before us and despite all odds, remained faithful to God. The writer calls them a great cloud of witnesses. Genealogies remind us that we are not alone.

Surely the genealogy of Jesus Christ reminds us that we are recipients of God's grace. The Messiah was born, not because of his ancestors, but in spite of them. Some of the names we read in this archive remind us of sordid and sad histories. Why does Matthew highlight the skeletons in the closet? Tamar, Rahab and Bathsheba were all women of questionable behaviour. Wicked kings are on the list, odd people to highlight in your family tree, for sure. Why not airbrush or gloss over these individuals? He is showing us that the grace of God is wide. His grace condescends to the lowest. His grace reaches to the Gentiles. The good news is, "But now in Christ Jesus ye who sometimes were far off are made nigh by the blood of Christ."[101]

Best of all we understand that Jesus Christ is the promised Messiah. Matthew presents his theme in the first verse, "This is the genealogy of Jesus the Messiah"[102] and in conclusion, "and Jacob the father of Joseph, the husband of Mary, and Mary was the mother of Jesus who is called the Messiah".[103] It is all about Jesus! It all points to Him.

---

[101] Ephesians 2:13 KJV
[102] Matthew 1:1 NIV
[103] Matthew 1:16 NIV

17

WITH GUSTO

"Oh, taste and see that the LORD is good! Blessed is the man who takes refuge in him!"

Psalm 34:8 NKJV

*P*refixes and suffixes, attached to the beginnings and endings of words, are useful little mechanisms. With the addition of two or three letters, they modify a word and create a new one. For example, the prefix "dis" negates a word: "agree" becomes "disagree". However, you may alight upon a word with a negative prefix which doesn't have a positive version. If you are disgusted, disgruntled, dismayed or disheveled, you're never going to be gusted, gruntled, mayed or sheveled. You don't say, "You're looking sheveled today" or "That gusts me". Words such as "disgusted" are negative words whose positive partners have disappeared or never existed in the first place. The origin of the word "disgust" is from the Latin verb "gustare" meaning "to taste". Later the Old French "desgouster" meaning distaste, in the sense of giving a bad taste to one's mouth, led to our English word in 1601. This was before the days of Shakespeare, who had to refer to "gorge rising" to capture the same emotion.

In Psalm 34:8, we are invited, "Oh, taste and see that the LORD is good! Blessed is the man who takes refuge in him!" [104] Another translation reads, "Open your mouth and taste, open your eyes and see how good God is. Blessed are you who run to him."[105] Another states, "Taste of His goodness".[106] The original Hebrew word for "taste" means "to try the flavour, to try something by experiencing it". The Hebrew

---

[104] Psalm 34:8 NKJV
[105] Psalm 34:8 MSG
[106] Psalm 34:8 The Voice

behind "see" means more than just observing what passes across our line of sight, but to perceive and envision, consider and discern. To taste and see is to experience. The Psalmist is inviting his readers to sample God's goodness for themselves and experience it in their lives.

In the previous verses of the Psalm, David has shared his own experience of God's goodness in delivering him from all his fears (v.4) in hearing his cries (v.6), and in saving him from all his troubles (v.6). Then after relating his own experience, David challenges the reader to personally experience God's goodness for himself or herself. If you look at the Psalms surrounding this one, you can see the flow of goodness in David's life – "Surely goodness and mercy shall follow me all the days of my life; and I will dwell in the house of the Lord forever."[107] "I would have lost heart, unless I had believed that I would see the goodness of the Lord in the land of the living."[108] "Oh, how great is Your goodness, which You have laid up for those who fear You, which You have prepared for those who trust in You in the presence of the sons of men!"[109]

As you taste and see that God is good, remember to do so "with gusto" (also from the word "gustare", to taste). "With gusto" means to partake with zest, zeal, ardour, to relish the experience. "Oh, thank God – he's so good! His love never runs out."[110]

---

[107] Psalm 23:6 NKJV
[108] Psalm 27:13 NKJV
[109] Psalm 31:19 KJV
[110] Psalm 107:1 MSG

18

DOG EARS

"But mark this: There will be terrible times in the last days."
2 Timothy 3:1 NIV

I have a confession to make: I dog-ear my books. In fact, I dog-ear a lot. I dog-ear every page that has something interesting on it and I dog-ear my last place in the book by folding down the top right corner and creasing it with my index finger to ensure it stays. I know this is a controversial action and you may grimace and call me sacrilegious. I have some particularly well-loved books that I have dog-eared and dog-eared and dog-eared some more. Those corners serve as a log of my reading journey and bookmark many remarkable discoveries. In my defence, evidence of dog-eared pages goes back all the way to Shakespeare's era, and even Sir Isaac Newton was known to dog-ear the pages of his journals and texts. If dog-earing pages is good enough for the man who discovered gravity, then surely it's permissible today.

It is important to bookmark certain things. For example, turn to 2 Timothy 3. The chapter begins with the words, "But mark this: There will be terrible times in the last days."[111]

Mark this. Paul wanted Timothy's attention. This was something he (and we) must know. He defined the very days in which we are living, distinguishing them with the descriptor "terrible". Other translations say "perilous" (NKJV), "very difficult" (NLT) and "perilous times of great stress and trouble [hard to deal with and hard to bear]" (AMPC). The Greek word is "chalepos". It is found in only one other place in the Bible (Matthew 8:28) where it is used to describe the two Gergesene demoniacs who met Jesus among the tombs. They were violent and dangerous. It reads, "When He had come to the other side, to the country

---

[111] 2 Timothy 3:1 NIV

of the Gergesenes, there met Him two demon-possessed men, coming out of the tombs, exceedingly fierce, so that no one could pass that way."[112]

The same word "chalepos" was used by Plutarch to describe what we would call an ugly, infected wound. It was also used by ancient astrological writers to describe a threatening conjunction of the heavenly bodies. Thus, behind the word is the idea of an environment besieged by danger and trouble. Demonic activity will be released in the last days that will bring about selfish, arrogant, abusive behaviour. Paul, in 2 Timothy 3:2, delineates ungodly characteristics typical of end times, launching with words, "For men will be lovers of themselves."[113] Comparing translations we get the description, "self-absorbed" (MSG), "love only themselves" (NLT), "narcissistic" (The Voice), "utterly self-centred" (AMPC). "Lovers of self" aptly heads the list since it is the essence of all ungodliness and the root from which all the other characteristics emanate. Jesus said in a pivotal verse, "If anyone would come after me, let him deny himself and take up his cross daily and follow me."[114]

The process of denial is humbly submitting to the will of God. This is our portfolio as a follower of Christ. Anything less than the absolute surrender of our lives to the lordship of Jesus Christ is eclipsing God of the glory He deserves. Though the days ahead may be "dangerous" let us "deny" ourselves and be determined to step forward as fearless followers of Jesus Christ.

---

[112] Matthew 8:28 NKJV
[113] 2 Timothy 3:2 NKJV
[114] Luke 9:23 ESV

19

BIRDS ON A WIRE

"And day after day they regularly assembled in the temple with united purpose"

Acts 4:46 AMPC

*B*irds perched on power lines are one of the mundane everyday scenes we often take for granted, yet one that prompts further probing. Surely I am not the only one with questions such as: Why do birds have a propensity to line up on power lines? Why have utility lines become avian hang-out spots? What did they do before human-strung wires were available? Given a choice of multiple wires, why do they congregate on the same one? Why do they usually face the same direction? How can they perch on high voltage wires without getting electrocuted? Or do they get shocked? Why do they sit spaced evenly in a row often facing the same direction? Why is it said that such a sight is a harbinger of bad weather? Who called this high-voltage meeting?

I have discovered the answer to some of these musings. The types of birds we see on power lines are called passerines (perching birds) and the reason they choose our man-made wires is because the high vantage point offers a bird's-eye view of surroundings and protects them from ground predators. Having no foliage to block the view gives them panoramic vision. The wires also serve as a staging area before a flock embarks on their seasonal odyssey of adventure. They perch in the same direction to face into the wind in order to reduce wind resistance. Their feathers are optimised for this direction of airflow and thus remain unruffled.

As I pondered this, I thought of how these birds daily demonstrate a lesson on vision and the advantage of seeing life from an "above" perspective. After their pattern we should position close to our "power source", embracing the wind of the Spirit. Essentially we should value their paradigm of togetherness. Hebrews 10:25 tells us, "not forsaking the assembling of ourselves together, as is the manner of some, but exhorting one another, and so much the more as you see the Day approaching".[115]

Christ circulates courage through community. He builds faith through fellowship. The Bible says, "As iron sharpens iron, so one person sharpens another."[116] Amazing things happen when disciples assemble. Consider the following excerpts of Scripture, "Then, the same day at evening, being the first day of the week, when the doors were shut where the disciples were assembled, for fear of the Jews, Jesus came and stood in the midst, and said to them, 'Peace be with you.'."[117] "And when they had prayed, the place where they were assembled together was shaken; and they were all filled with the Holy Spirit, and they spoke the word of God with boldness."[118] "And when the day of Pentecost had fully come, they were all assembled together in one place, when suddenly there came a sound from heaven like the rushing of a violent tempest blast, and it filled the whole house in which they were sitting"[119] and "And day after day they regularly assembled in the temple with united purpose".[120]

May we harness the import of united purpose and align on purpose for purpose.

---

[115] Hebrews 10:25 NKJV
[116] Proverbs 27:17 NIV
[117] John 20:19 NKJV
[118] Acts 4:31 NKJV
[119] Acts 2:1–2 AMPC
[120] Acts 4:26 AMPC

20

UNFURLED

"You have unfurled a banner for those who revere You, a signal to gather in safety out of the enemy's reach."

Psalm 60:4 (VOICE)

A national flag is one of the most instantly recognizable symbols of a country's identity. The design and colour of a flag symbolically help identify a country's values, beliefs, geography and history. A vexillologist, a person who studies flags, can reveal many epic details. Did you know that there are only two countries with square flags? They are Switzerland and Vatican City. Did you know that the most uncommon colour found on a flag is purple? It is only used on two flags of the world. Purple often represents royalty or richness, so it is surprising that it isn't used on more flags today. Did you know that when the Queen is in residence at Buckingham Palace the Royal Standard is flown on the rooftop flagpole? However, when the Queen is not there the Union Flag (Union Jack) will be flown instead. Did you know that the first Olympic flag went missing for seventy-seven years after the 1920 games until a 1920 Olympian revealed he'd had it in his suitcase the whole time?

The reason I embarked on an odyssey of flag facts was because the Bible says, "The Lord is my Banner"[121] or in Hebrew, "Jehovah Nissi". The word "Nissi" is derived from the Hebrew (nes) which means a flag, a signal, a banner, a standard, an ensign. Exodus 17:15 tells us, "Moses built an altar and called it 'The Lord is my Banner.'"[121]

A banner is something that identifies and unifies a particular group of people. A banner also functions as a rallying point for troops in a battle. To stand behind a banner means to identify with its cause. A banner also marks conquest. In Exodus 15 the Israelites had won the

---

[121] Exodus 17:15 NIV

battle with the Lord as their banner. It was the Lord whose banner they followed into battle and the Lord is the one who claims the victory.

The Lord is our Banner because we live to celebrate and honour His faithfulness to us, unfurled in myriad ways, from the rising sun to the risen Christ. We pledge our allegiance to Him. He is our banner because He gives us identity – we know whose we are, and whom we serve. We submit to His values. He is our Banner because He is our focal point and we rally to Him. We trust and know that the Lord fights for us. The Bible states, "When the enemy comes in like a flood, the Spirit of the Lord will lift up a standard against him."[122] As we muster for battle, we rely on Him for victory. "Some trust in chariots and some in horses, but we trust in the name of the Lord our God".[123] His Name is Jehovah Nissi. Isaiah prophetically stated, "And in that day there shall be a Root of Jesse, who shall stand as a banner to the people."[124]

He is Jesus, the Lord our Banner. Don't try to fight your own battles in your own strength. In and through Him you are an overcomer, or as Paul phrased it, "No, in all these things we are more than conquerors through him who loved us."[125] In another translation it reads, "But no matter what comes, we will always taste victory through Him who loved us."[126]

---

[122] Isaiah 59:19 NKJV
[123] Psalm 20:7 NIV
[124] Isaiah 11:10 NKJV
[125] Romans 8:37 NIV
[126] Romans 8:37 VOICE

21

HOW MANY IS A PLETHORA?

"that you may be filled with all the fullness of God."
Ephesians 3:19 NKJV

ow many is a plethora? The *Cambridge Dictionary* defines "plethora" as "a very large amount of something, especially a larger amount than you need, want, or can deal with." [127] Its synonyms are: deluge, profusion, superabundance, surplus, overflow. Antonyms are: want, barrenness or lack. It can have negative connotations, for example, "The town has been blighted with a plethora of empty shops." "Plethora" is derived from the Greek word for "fullness" (pleroma). Paul used this word and its conjugates ("pleroo", to fill, to cause to abound, to furnish or supply liberally). The word "pleroma", according to *Strong's Concordance*, can refer to "a ship inasmuch as it is filled (i.e., manned) with sailors, rowers, and soldiers" or in the New Testament it is applied to "the body of believers, as that which is filled with the presence, power, agency, riches of God and of Christ". [128]

A good example of its usage is Ephesians 3:19 which speaks of being "filled with all the fullness of God" [129] or "pleroo" with the "pleroma" of God. Another translation reads, "Live full lives, full in the fullness of God." [130] Check out the context in the Passion Translation, "Then you will be empowered to discover what every holy one experiences – the great magnitude of the astonishing love of Christ in all its dimensions. How deeply intimate and far-reaching is His love! How enduring and inclusive it is! Endless love beyond measurement that transcends our

---

[127] www.dictionary.cambridge.org
[128] *Strong's Concordance* G4138
[129] Ephesians 3:19 NKJV
[130] Ephesians 3:19 MSG

understanding – this extravagant love pours into you until you are filled to overflowing with the fullness of God!"[131]

May His extravagant love pour into us until we are filled to overflowing with the fullness of God! The Amplified Bible states, "that you may be filled [through all your being] unto all the fullness of God [may have the richest measure of the divine Presence, and become a body wholly filled and flooded with God Himself]!"[132]

God created you and designed you to run at optimal level when you are filled with His love. We can be filled with a number of things. Have you ever met a guy who was full of "himself"? We can be full of a myriad of negative things: resentful, fearful, doubtful, ungrateful, deceitful, boastful, scornful etc … What does your overflow say you are full of today?

If you allow yourself to be filled with God, you cannot be filled with self at the same time. May His extravagant love pour into you until you are filled to overflowing with the fullness of God. There is no limit placed upon the plenitude that can be ours except that which we ourselves make. For we shall be filled according to the measure of our appropriation and our communion with the fountainhead. God is love, so we must long for that same brand of agape love to permeate our whole beings. May we indeed have the richest measure of the divine Presence, and become a body wholly filled and flooded with God Himself.

---

[131] Ephesians 3:18–19 TPT
[132] Ephesians 3:19 AMPC

22

COWS IN CONCRETE

"Brethren, join in following my example"
                                    Philippians 3:17 NKJV

ecently I had the joy of revisiting with my family a place where many happy childhood memories were forged. As we strolled along a pathway leading into the mountains, one particular memory flooded back. It was of the day when the very path we trod was being laid. I had been gathering wild flowers nearby and was keeping an eye on proceedings. No sooner had the wet concrete been poured out, and the workers departed, when I spotted a number of unrestrained bovines stomping along and leaving their heavy imprints. Multiple large hoof marks were firmly embedded in the concrete for posterity. It was those very imprints that I noticed on our walk.

The experience reminded me of the Greek word "tupos", a very interesting word. In the Bible "tupos" is translated as "example", "model" or "pattern". It literally refers to a visible mark or impression made by an instrument or object. A classic example is when Thomas doubted Jesus' resurrection from the dead, declaring, "Unless I see in His hands the print of the nails, and put my finger into the print of the nails, and put my hand into His side, I will not believe." The word "print" is "tupos".

Tupos can also refer to a "model" or "mould" into which clay or wax is pressed, so that it might take the exact shape of the mould. It can mean the impression left by a seal or the stamp of a coin. Have you ever tried taking a coin, putting a piece of paper on top of it and rubbing back and forth across the surface of the underlying coin using the side of a pencil lead until an impression of the coin begins to appear?

In 1 Thessalonians 1 :7 Paul praises the Thessalonians for having become "a model" for other churches. He says, "You became a model to all the believers in Macedonia and Achaia."[133] He told Titus, "Show yourself in all respects to be a model of good works."[134] How? "Titus, you have to set a good example for everyone. Go out of your way to do what is right, speak the truth with the weight and authority that come from an honest and pure life. No one can argue with that. Then your enemies will cower in shame because they have nothing bad to say against us."[135] Timothy was to show himself an example (a tupos) as well, "Let no one look down on your youthfulness, but rather in speech, conduct, love, faith and purity, show yourself an example of those who believe."[136]

Paul's exhortation to the Philippians is noteworthy, "My beloved friends, imitate my walk with God and follow all those who walk according to the way of life we modelled before you."[137] The bottom line is this – you make an impression on people. Are you a model of good works? Would an exhibit of your speech, conduct, love, faith and purity be an example worth emulating? Does your example reflect your walk with God? May it show a concrete example of what God is like.

---

[133] 1 Thessalonians 1:7 NIV
[134] Titus 2:7 ESV
[135] Titus 2:7–8 VOICE
[136] 1 Timothy 4:12 NASB
[137] Philippians 3:17 TPT

23

SIGNS FOLLOWING

"And truly Jesus did many other signs in the presence of His disciples, which are not written in this book; but these are written that you may believe that Jesus is the Christ, the Son of God, and that believing you may have life in His name."

John 20:30–31 NKJV

John tells us that Jesus did "many other signs".[138] Jesus' signs are recorded in the Bible for a purpose. We are told what it is: "But these are written that you may believe that Jesus is the Christ, the Son of God, and that believing you may have life in His name." [139] The word "sign" is a translation of the Greek word "semeion". In ancient history, this word represented the official written notice announcing the final verdict of a court. It also described the signature or seal applied to a document to guarantee its authenticity. Thus "semeion" came to be an authenticating mark or guarantee of something. The "signs" of Jesus were supernatural acts of God's stamp of approval on His ministry and message.

John introduces us to Jesus' first sign, "This beginning of signs Jesus did in Cana of Galilee, and manifested His glory; and His disciples believed in Him."[140] In this sign He manifested His glory. In the next chapter John records, "Now when He was in Jerusalem at the Passover, during the feast, many believed in His name when they saw the signs which He did."[141] John tells us of how Nicodemus came to Jesus at night and said to Him, "Rabbi, we know that You are a teacher come from God; for no one can do these signs that You do unless God is with

---

138 John 20:3o NKJV
139 John 20:31 NKJV
140 John 2:11 NKJV
141 John 2:23 NKJV

him."[142] Moments before Jesus ascended to the Father, He told the disciples, "And these signs will follow those who believe".[143] Jesus was sending His disciples into the world to preach the Gospel. As He sent them forth, He said that God's authenticating stamp of approval would be upon their ministry. The "signs" that followed them that believe the official declaration that they were God-sent and that the Gospel message was true. We are told, "And they went out and preached everywhere, the Lord working with them and confirming the word through the accompanying signs. Amen."[144] In the early church we read, "Then fear came upon every soul, and many wonders and signs were done through the apostles."[145] Again, "At the hands of the apostles many signs and wonders were taking place among the people".[146] Widespread healings occurred, and multitudes continued to believe and be added to the Lord. Notice the ministry of Stephen: "And Stephen, full of faith and power, did great wonders and signs among the people."[147] In Acts 8 we are told that Philip went down to a city in Samaria and proclaimed the Messiah there. Verse 6 states, "When the crowds heard Philip and saw the signs he performed, they all paid close attention to what he said."[148]

As a believer, are you seeing the supernatural signature of God on your life and ministry? God wants to confirm His word with signs following. He wants to manifest His glory so that others may believe and have life in His Name.

---

[142] John 3:2 NKJV
[143] Mark 16:17 NKJV
[144] Mark 16:20 NKJV
[145] Acts 2:43 NKJV
[146] Acts 5:12NKJV
[147] Acts 6:8 NKJV
[148] Acts 8:6 NIV

24

IT'S HOW YOU CARRY IT

"Take My yoke upon you and learn from Me"
Matthew 11:29 NKJV

*S*omeone once quipped, "It's not the load that breaks you down. It's the way you carry it." Are you carrying a heavy load of work, emotions, or another stressor in life? Recently I have found that there are so many things to do and not enough hours in the day to do them. I have prayed: Do I need to lighten the load? What needs to go? Then a friend on social media shared this, "It's not the load but how you carry it. In the new era many will not change what they do, but they will be transformed by how they carry it."

It's the way you carry it. Have you ever tried to lift something cumbersome and weighty? It seemed like an impossible task and you had to resort to dragging it. Then someone came along and with a little flexing and correct posture carried it to its intended destination. Again, it's not the load but how you carry it. Try shifting furniture on your own and you will know that it's not an easy undertaking. But when someone takes hold of the other end, it's undemanding. The Bible tells us, "Cast your burden upon the LORD and He will sustain you; He will never allow the righteous to be shaken."[149] David wrote, "Commit your way to the Lord [roll and repose each care of your load on Him]".[150] When George Mueller was asked how he could be so settled in the middle of a hectic day with so many uncertainties in the orphanage, he answered, "I rolled sixty things onto the Lord this morning."[151] Like David he knew the truth, "Blessed be the Lord, who daily bears our burden, The God

---

[149] Psalm 55:22 NASB
[150] Psalm 37:5 AMPC
[151] George Mueller, "The Satisfied Soul", 308

who is our salvation. Selah."[152] Or, as another translation phrases it, "Blessed be the Lord who carries our heavy loads every day, the True God who is our salvation."[153] Jesus says to us, "Come to Me, all you who labor and are heavy laden, and I will give you rest. Take My yoke upon you and learn from Me, for I am gentle and lowly in heart, and you will find rest for your souls. For My yoke is easy and My burden is light."[154]

A yoke is something Jesus would have made in a carpenter's shop. It is a wooden frame joining two oxen at the neck, enabling them to pull a plough or cart together. Linked by a yoke, the two oxen could work together, pulling whatever burden was attached to the yoke. The function of the yoke is to provide greater strength and make the burden easier to carry. When ancient farmers trained a new ox, they would often yoke the young animal beside a stronger, more experienced ox. This pairing would bear the burden of the workload and help guide the younger animal through the learning process. I love the way Eugene Peterson translates this passage in *The Message*: "Walk with me and work with me – watch how I do it. Learn the unforced rhythms of grace. I won't lay anything heavy or ill-fitting on you. Keep company with me and you'll learn to live freely and lightly." (vv.29–30). Are you walking with Him and working with Him? Are you watching how He does it? Are you learning the unforced rhythms of grace? Are you keeping company with Him and learning to live freely and lightly?

---

[152] Psalm 68:19 NASB
[153] Psalm 68:19 VOICE
[154] Matthew 11:28–30 NIV

25

LET HIS MINDSET BE YOUR MOTIVATION

"Be free from pride-filled opinions, for they will only harm your cherished unity. Don't allow self-promotion to hide in your hearts, but in authentic humility put others first and view others as more important than yourselves. Abandon every display of selfishness. Possess a greater concern for what matters to others instead of your own interests. And consider the example that Jesus, the Anointed One, has set before us. Let his mindset become your motivation."

Philippians 2:3–5 TPT

Let his mindset become your motivation. Or, in another translation, "Let this mind be in you which was also in Christ Jesus".[155] I recently came across the words, "Mindset is what separates the best from the rest." [156] When addressing the Corinthians, Paul spoke of having "the mind of Christ". The phrase "mind of Christ" or "mind of the Lord" comes from Isaiah 40:13, "Who comprehends the mind of the Lord, or gives him instruction as his counselor?" [157] Paul cites this reference in 1 Corinthians 2:16, then discloses the most amazing truth, "For 'who has known the mind of the Lord that he may instruct Him?' But we have the mind of Christ."[158]

But we have the mind of Christ. The Amplified Bible states, "For who has known or understood the mind (the counsels and purposes) of the Lord so as to guide and instruct Him and give Him knowledge? But

---

[155] Philippians 2:5 NKJV
[156] Jo Owen, *The Mindset of Success: From Good Management to Great Leadership*
[157] Isaiah 40:13 NET
[158] 1 Corinthians 2:16 NKJV

we have the mind of Christ (the Messiah) and do hold the thoughts (feelings and purposes) of His heart."[159]

Your mindset comes from where your mind is set. Paul encourages the Colossian believers to "set your minds and keep them set on what is above (the higher things), not on the things that are on the earth".[160] He tells us, "For those who live according to the flesh set their minds on the things of the flesh, but those who live according to the Spirit set their minds on the things of the Spirit. For to set the mind on the flesh is death, but to set the mind on the Spirit is life and peace."[161]

Our minds need to be consistently renewed, moving away from the mind of the flesh and into the mindset of Christ. Still speaking to the Romans, Paul writes, "Be transformed by the renewal of your mind".[162] Renewal, in the original language, speaks of renovating. We need to "take every thought captive to obey Christ".[163] The mind of Christ stands in stark contrast with the wisdom of the world. With the mind of Christ we desire to bring glory to God. We have a longing to seek and save the lost. We have a prayerful dependence on God. In today's verse, having the mind of Christ consists of a spirit of humility, having a servant's attitude of self-sacrifice and an interest in the welfare of others. Take some time today to honestly assess in which direction your mind is typically set. Why not use the lyrics written by Kate B Wilkinson (1925) as your prayer:

May the mind of Christ, my Savior,
Live in me from day to day,
By His love and power controlling
All I do and say.

---

159 1 Corinthians 2:16 AMPC
160 Colossians 3:2 AMPC
161 Romans 8:5 ESV
162 Romans 12:2 ESV
163 2 Corinthians 10:5 ESV

26

CHEER UP!

"I have told you these things, so that in Me you may have [perfect] peace and confidence. In the world you have tribulation and trials and distress and frustration; but be of good cheer [take courage; be confident, certain, undaunted]! For I have overcome the world. [I have deprived it of power to harm you and have conquered it for you.]"

John 16:33 AMPC

*J*esus wants you and I to have perfect peace and confidence[164], found exclusively as we rest in Him. In John 14:27, Jesus clearly states that the peace He gives is "not as the world gives".[165] We know, as He said, that in the world there is "tribulation and trials and distress and frustration".[166] Those words surely ring true in our day, but He goes on to say that we, rather than getting distressed and frustrated, should "be of good cheer".[167] We should "take courage; be confident, certain and undaunted".[168]

Another translation states, "In the world you will have tribulation; but be of good cheer, I have overcome the world."[169] I am so thankful that there is not a full stop after the word "tribulation", rather a semi-colon, followed by the encouraging words, "But be of good cheer". Jesus assures His disciples, "I have overcome the world". The word "overcome" is a translation of the Greek word "nikao", which means "to come off victorious". Notice, He doesn't say, "I will overcome the world." Instead, He uses a perfect tense verb which refers to a past act

---

[164] John 16:33 AMPC
[165] John 14:27 NKJV
[166] John 16:33 AMPC
[167] John 16:33 AMPC
[168] John 16:33 AMPC
[169] John 16:33 NKJV

with abiding results. The grammar of the original Greek doesn't simply refer to a single victory; rather, it conveys a continuous, abiding victory both now and hereafter. Through Christ you are an overcomer; you are more than a conqueror through Him. Overwhelming victory is ours through Christ.[170] Aren't you glad Jesus "told you these things"?[171] What a difference they make! Be of good cheer. Or as the Living Bible says, cheer up, "I have told you all this so that you will have peace of heart and mind. Here on earth you will have many trials and sorrows; but cheer up, for I have overcome the world."[172]

Jesus had spoken the words "Be of good cheer" to a paralytic, brought to Jesus by four friends. We read, "When Jesus saw their faith, He said to the paralytic, 'Son, be of good cheer; your sins are forgiven you.'."[173] Speaking to the woman who pressed through the crowd to touch the hem of His garment, He said, "'Be of good cheer, daughter; your faith has made you well.' And the woman was made well from that hour."[174] Again, addressing the disciples in the midst of a storm, He spoke to them saying, "Be of good cheer! It is I; do not be afraid."[175] He says the same words to us today. Be of good cheer. Take courage! Be confident! Remain certain! Continue undaunted!

---

[170] Romans 8:37 NLT
[171] John 16:33 AMPC
[172] John 16:33 LB
[173] Matthew 9:2 NJKV
[174] Matthew 9:22 NKJV
[175] Matthew 14:27 NKJV

27

CLOUD NINE

"Blessed are the poor in spirit, for theirs is the kingdom of heaven. Blessed are those who mourn, for they will be comforted. Blessed are the meek, for they will inherit the earth. Blessed are those who hunger and thirst for righteousness, for they will be filled."
Matthew 5:3–6 NIV

*I*f you wish to express elation or euphoria, you might refer to being "over the moon", "on top of the world", "walking on sunshine", "walking on air", "full of the joys of spring" or you might say that you are "on cloud nine". To be on cloud nine is to be extremely happy and full of bliss. But where did such an idiom originate? The origin can be found in the *International Cloud Atlas* from 1896. In 1890, a group of meteorologists from various countries assembled and they attempted to establish an international cloud classification system. They agreed on ten classes, or levels. The cumulonimbus cloud became cloud nine. These clouds, as I know from living in Northern Ireland, are associated with rain showers and thunderstorms. In fact, they were called thunder clouds or shower clouds. But they are the biggest and fluffiest, perfect for sitting on. This cloud often rises to forty thousand feet; and when you are on such a cloud, you are literally on top of the world.

"Nine" has significance in the Bible. It is recorded that Jesus Christ, the son of God, died exactly at "the ninth hour".[176] In 1 Corinthians 12:8–10 Paul mentions nine gifts of the Spirit. Galatians, the ninth book of the New Testament, tells us of the fruit of the Spirit (Galatians 5:22, 23) mentioning nine qualities: love, joy, peace, longsuffering, kindness, goodness, faithfulness, gentleness, self-control.[177] In Matthew 5:3–12

---

[176] Mark 15:34 ESV
[177] Galatians 5:22, 23 NKJV

there are nine Beatitudes, which Jesus spoke in His Sermon on the Mount. Each of them starts with the word "blessed".

I want to draw your attention to how the Amplified Bible translates the Greek word "makarios" for "blessed". Let's see its full flavour. It reads, "Blessed (happy, to be envied, and spiritually prosperous – with life-joy and satisfaction in God's favor and salvation, regardless of their outward conditions) are the poor in spirit".[178] "Blessed and enviably happy [with a happiness produced by the experience of God's favor and especially conditioned by the revelation of His matchless grace] are those who mourn".[179]

"Makarios" is an adjective, a description of a state of being. The idea behind "makarios" is that something is made "large" or "lengthy". When God "blesses" us, He "extends" His benefits to us, conferring advantages and endowing us with contentedness. He "enlarges" His mercy to us. He "lengthens" His charity in our direction. It is a grace word expressing the special joys and satisfaction granted the person who experiences salvation. We deserved nothing but judgment and the results of the curse, but on the cross Jesus bore the curse that was upon humanity and died in our place. Because of the redemptive work of Christ, we can now receive the blessing of God through faith in Christ. Why settle for "cloud nine" when you can experience heavenly blessing?

---

[178] Matthew 5:3 AMPC
[179] Matthew 5:4 AMPC

28

LOVERS OF GOD

"But know this, that in the last days perilous times will come: For men will be lovers of themselves, lovers of money, boasters, proud, blasphemers, disobedient to parents, unthankful, unholy, unloving, unforgiving, slanderers, without self-control, brutal, despisers of good, traitors, headstrong, haughty, lovers of pleasure rather than lovers of God, having a form of godliness but denying its power. And from such people turn away!"

2 Timothy 3:1–5 NKJV

Four times the word "lovers" is used in 1 Timothy 3:1–5. The passage of Scripture speaks of people being "lovers of themselves, lovers of money" [180] and "lovers of pleasure rather than lovers of God". [181] Let's zoom in on the latter phrase, "lovers of pleasure rather than lovers of God".

The words "lovers of pleasure" are a translation of one Greek word: "philodonos", a compound of two words, "phileo" and "hedonos". It forecasts that people in the last days will be preoccupied with pleasure and live for the gratification of their flesh and the pursuit of their own personal happiness. It's the origin of the English word "hedonism", synonyms of which are carnality, self-indulgence, debauchery and gratification. Jesus, speaking of seed falling on different soils, mentioned thorny ground and referred to the danger of the pleasures of life, "Now the ones that fell among thorns are those who, when they have heard, go out and are choked with cares, riches, and pleasures of life, and bring no fruit to maturity." [182]

---

[180] 2 Timothy 3:2 NKJV
[181] 2 Timothy 3:4 NKJV
[182] Luke 8:14 NKJV

The pleasures of life can choke and hinder the Word of God sown in our lives. The writer of Hebrews held Moses up as an example when he said that he chose "rather to suffer affliction with the people of God than to enjoy the passing pleasures of sin".[183] Notice how being a lover of pleasure is in contrast to being a lover of God, "lovers of pleasure rather than lovers of God". The words "rather than" are a translation of the Greek word "mallon", which draws a drastic comparison between two points. It implies that something is extremely different in comparison to something else. Another translation states, "[They will be] lovers of sensual pleasures and vain amusements more than and rather than lovers of God."[184] Notice also that those who are lovers of pleasure can hold to a form of godliness. But because they are not truly "lovers of God", they are denying His power (dunamis) and refusing to walk in His ways. The words "lovers of God" in Greek is one word, "philotheos", picturing people who are deeply and profoundly in love with God. Jesus said that at the end of the age "the love of many will grow cold"[185] but that does not have to be our condition. Rather, He said, "You shall love the Lord your God with all your heart, with all your soul, and with all your mind."[186] In reality, loving the Lord your God with all your heart, soul, mind and strength is simply a response. For we love because He first loved us. Don't miss this: the Bible tells us, "There's a private place reserved for the lovers of God, where they sit near him and receive the revelation-secrets of his promises."[187]

---

[183] Hebrews 11:25 NKJV
[184] 2 Timothy 3:4 AMPC
[185] Matthew 24:12 NKJV
[186] Matthew 22:37 NKJV
[187] Matthew 22:37 NKJV

29

WISDOM OF WOMBATS

"Do you want to be counted wise, to build a reputation for wisdom?"

James 3:13 MSG

While in possession of the remote control one night I came across a nature documentary on wombats. What adorable, amazing creatures they are! I'm bursting to share a few extraordinary facts with you about these short-legged, stocky marsupials. For starters, they poop cubes! Yes, you read that correctly. The neat, cube-shaped packages are deposited to mark territory and don't roll away. Although wombats look pudgy and walk with an awkward waddle, when threatened they can sustain speeds of twenty-five miles per hour for ninety seconds. That's almost as fast as Olympic sprinter Usain Bolt whose top speed was recorded at a little less than twenty-eight miles per hour. These muscular quadrupedal creatures are also top-notch diggers, excavating their extensive network of underground tunnels and chambers. Like other marsupials, wombats have pouches where their newborns continue their development. However, a wombat's pouch has a special difference – it faces backwards, opening toward the mother's rear rather than her head. This prevents dirt and debris from entering while digging. Don't let their unassuming posterior fool you. One of the wombat's primary defences is its toughened butt, which is mostly made of cartilage and covered with tough thick skin. When a predator approaches, a wombat dives headfirst into a nearby burrow, blocking off the entrance with its rump. Digestive tract morphology of wombats shows that it takes a wombat up to two weeks to digest a meal. Finally, here's a fact worth dwelling on – a gathering of Vombatidae, alias wombats, is known as a wisdom.

A wisdom of wombats. Isn't it "wisdom" to assemble together and work together? The Bible tells us, "And let us consider one another in order to stir up love and good works, not forsaking the assembling of ourselves together, as is the manner of some, but exhorting one another, and so much the more as you see the Day approaching."[188]

A unified, harmonious church presents a powerful witness to the world. In the wisdom literature of the Bible, we read, "As iron sharpens iron, so one person sharpens another."[189] Paul had to address a lack of wisdom evident among the Corinthian people stating, "For where there are envy, strife, and divisions among you, are you not carnal and behaving like mere men? For when one says, 'I am of Paul,' and another, 'I am of Apollos,' are you not carnal? Who then is Paul, and who is Apollos, but ministers through whom you believed, as the Lord gave to each one? I planted, Apollos watered, but God gave the increase … For we are God's fellow workers."[190] Or, "For we are fellow workmen (joint promoters, laborers together) with and for God."[191]

Together in unity we can accomplish more. May we operate in wisdom from above. James spoke of it asking, "Do you want to be counted wise, to build a reputation for wisdom?"[192] He gave us timely advice worth pondering, "Whenever you're trying to look better than others or get the better of others, things fall apart and everyone ends up at the other's throats. Real wisdom, God's wisdom, begins with a holy life and is characterised by getting along with others. It is gentle and reasonable, overflowing with mercy and blessings, not hot one day and cold the next, not two-faced. You can develop a healthy, robust community that lives right with God and enjoy its results only if you do the hard work of getting along with each other, treating each other with dignity and honor."[193]

---

[188] Hebrews 10:24–25 NKJV
[189] Proverbs 27:17 NIV
[190] 1 Corinthians 3:3–7 ,9 NKJV
[191] 1 Corinthians 3:9 AMPC
[192] James 3:13 MSG
[193] James 3:16–18 MSG

30

YOUR SPIRITUAL SPECTACLES

"So be very careful how you live, not being like those with no understanding, but live honorably with true wisdom, for we are living in evil times. Take full advantage of every day as you spend your life for his purposes."

Ephesians 5:16–17 TPT

ake full advantage of every day as you spend your life for His purposes. To do so, we need to walk as the wise. Paul says, "So be very careful how you live".[194] Or, "walk circumspectly"[195] as another translation renders it. The English word "circumspectly" is now deemed archaic, but there is something engaging and charming about it. It derives from the Latin "circum" (around) and "specere" (to look – the origin of the word "spectacles"). We are to walk with spiritual spectacles on, carefully staying on the path set by God. To use a personal example, the world looks very different for me depending upon the prescription lenses, or glasses, through which I look. I have a pair for fine reading and another pair for long-distance visibility. If I pick up the wrong pair my view is distorted and it is difficult to see the path ahead.

When we see to it that we are walking circumspectly we are conforming to His Word, attuned to His will and seeing everything through His eyes and from His perspective. A question worth asking is this: By whose perspective are you living life? Is it a perspective being influenced by the common assumptions of culture? Is it a philosophy that is built upon human wisdom? Be careful! The lenses through which you view life will dramatically affect the way you spend your life. The Greek word which translates as "circumspectly" is "akribos", meaning

---

[194] Ephesians 5:16 TPT
[195] Ephesians 5:16 KJV

"characterised by accuracy, exactness, thoroughness and precision". Paul has already told the Ephesians to "walk worthy of the calling with which you were called",[196] to "walk not as other Gentiles walk",[197] to "walk in love",[198] to "walk as children of light"[199] and now, "walk circumspectly" (5:15).

Tread gingerly; be mindful of your steps as you would if negotiating a minefield. Closely watch the parameters within which you are to regulate your life. The Amplified Bible states, "Look carefully then how you walk! Live purposefully and worthily and accurately, not as the unwise and witless, but as wise (sensible, intelligent people)." I love this translation because it prompts a daily audit: Am I living purposefully today? Am I living worthily? Am I living accurately? Proverbs 4:26–27 tells us, "Consider well the path of your feet, and let all your ways be established and ordered aright. Turn not aside to the right hand or to the left; remove your foot from evil."[200]

Take full advantage of every day as you spend your life for His purposes. As you step out today, what opportunities are yours? Each day is an opportunity to make a difference in someone else's life. Galatians 6:10 says, "Take advantage of every opportunity to be a blessing to others".[201]

Take full advantage of the God-given opportunities. We may be "living in evil times" but with an eternal perspective we can make the most of every living and breathing moment. I hate to admit it, but I have waived and wasted too many kairos moments. Preoccupied with my own predicaments, I have time and again failed to discern God's promptings. But today is a new day to redeem the time.

---

[196] Ephesians 4:1 NKJV
[197] Ephesians 4:17 KJV
[198] Ephesians 5:2 KJV
[199] Ephesians 5:8 KJV
[200] Proverbs 4:26–27 AMPC
[201] Galatians 6:10

31

IN HIS GRIP

"Behold, God is my helper and ally; the Lord is my upholder"

Psalm 54:4 AMPC

I remember back to the days when I had to cross a busy road with small children in tow. I put out my hand and said, "Hold on tight", and my little ones grasped my hand as tightly as they could. However, I never depended on their grasp. It is my grip on their hand that held them and kept them secure. Our Father whispers, "Hold tight" as we navigate the thoroughfares of life, but it is His grasp that assures our safe passage.

Isn't it reassuring to know that He holds your hand and upholds your life? David acknowledged, "Behold, God is my helper and ally; the Lord is my upholder".[202] It is such a comfort to know the reality of this truth. God speaks to galvanise the hearts of His people, "Do not yield to fear, for I am always near. Never turn your gaze from me, for I am your faithful God. I will infuse you with my strength and help you in every situation. I will hold you firmly with my victorious right hand."[203] A few verses later, the reassurance is reiterated, "I am Yahweh, your mighty God! I grip your right hand and won't let you go! I whisper to you: 'Don't be afraid; I am here to help you!'."[204] Psalm 139 celebrates the amazing attributes of God's omniscience (v.1–6) and omnipresence (v. 7–12). In His omniscience God knows our every movement. He perceives our thoughts and is acquainted with all our ways and words. In His omnipresence He is with us wherever we find ourselves. This is especially evident in verses 9–11: "If I take the wings of the morning, and dwell in the uttermost parts of the sea, even there Your hand shall

---

[202] Psalm 54:4 AMPC
[203] Isaiah 41:10 TPT
[204] Isaiah 41:13 TPT

lead me, and Your right hand shall hold me."[205] "Even there" in the remotest location, in the uttermost part of the globe, "even there Your hand shall lead me, and Your right hand shall hold me."

David, celebrating the heritage of the righteous stated, "But the Lord upholds the righteous …The steps of a good man are ordered by the Lord, and He delights in his way. Though he fall, he shall not be utterly cast down; for the Lord upholds him with His hand."[206] When he was in the wilderness of Judah David penned these words, "My soul follows close behind You; Your right hand upholds me."[207]

You may find yourself in a wilderness situation right now, but God wants you to know that He has your hand. Moving into the New Testament, we read, "He [God] Himself has said, 'I will not in any way fail you nor give you up nor leave you without support. [I will] not, [I will] not, [I will] not in any degree leave you helpless nor forsake nor let [you] down (relax My hold on you)! [Assuredly not!]' So, we take comfort and are encouraged and confidently and boldly say, The Lord is my Helper; I will not be seized with alarm [I will not fear or dread or be terrified]. What can man do to me?"[208]

He will not leave you without support. He will not leave you helpless. He will not relax His hold on you. Or as another translation renders it, "I will never leave you alone, never! And I will not loosen my grip on your life!"[209] God has clearly promised to stay with us and support us every step of the way. You are in His grip.

---

[205] Psalm 139:9–11 NKJV
[206] Psalm 37:17, 23–24 NKJV
[207] Psalm 63:8 NKJV
[208] Hebrews 13:5–6 AMPC
[209] Hebrews 13:5 TPT

32

CLARITY WITH CHARITY

"Then we will no longer be infants, tossed back and forth by the waves, and blown here and there by every wind of teaching and by the cunning and craftiness of people in their deceitful scheming. Instead, speaking the truth in love, we will grow to become in every respect the mature body of him who is the head, that is, Christ."

Ephesians 4:14–15 NIV

Notice the words, "speaking the truth in love".[210] "What is truth?"[211] or in Latin, "Quid est Veritas?" asked Pilate, a question countless others have reiterated through the centuries, as if truth is subject to human interpretation. Interestingly, the one to whom Pilate addressed the question "What is truth?" was Jesus, the One who is "the way and the truth and the life".[212] He is the very personification of Truth. Before Pilate stood the One "full of grace and truth".[213] Before him stood the One of whom John wrote, "grace and truth came through Jesus Christ".[214] Before Him stood the One who had already uttered the words, "If you abide in my word, you are truly my disciples, and you will know the truth, and the truth will set you free."[215]

Knowing the truth freed the disciples from deceptions, errors and heresies. On the night before His crucifixion Jesus defined truth for us, stating, "Thy Word is Truth."[216] The Bible is the inspired Word of God – Truth with a capital T. The challenge is that we live in a culture where

---

[210] Ephesians 4:15 NIV
[211] John 18:38 NIV
[212] John 14:6 NIV
[213] John 1:14 ESV
[214] John 1:17 ESV
[215] John 8:31–32 ESV
[216] John 17:17 KJV

tolerance has been elevated above truth. But regardless of the challenges made against it, the Word of God is the only true, sure and solid foundation for us to build our lives and ministry upon. As believers we need to "stand firm with the belt of truth" tightly buckled around our waists.[217] One of the last things Paul told Timothy was, "Do your best to present yourself to God as one approved, a worker who does not need to be ashamed and who correctly handles the word of truth." Note the phrase "correctly handles the word of truth".[218] In writing to the Ephesians Paul made it clear that we are to speak the truth in love. Truth is coupled with love. First, we are to speak the truth. Second, we are to do so in a way that is characterised by love. The context of Paul's instruction centres around doctrinal issues and is directly applicable to the edification of fellow believers. We are to speak the truth, then, in contrast to the falsehood of deceptive teachings and worldly philosophies; and we are to do so in love, for the purpose of building up the body of Christ.

Check the content of what you say – are you upholding the truth of God's revealed Word?

Monitor the manner in which you speak the truth – you are called to communicate in such a way that our speaking honours our Lord Jesus and edifies His body, the church. Biblical love is definitely not soft on sin, error, or false teaching; but it is softened with compassion and seasoned with grace in the way it interacts with other people. With the two parameters in place, truth and love, may we make the most of every word that we speak, type or tweet. What we say and why has such a huge impact.

---

[217] Ephesians 6:14 NIV
[218] 2 Timothy 2:15

33

A BOW RELEASED

"Be still and rest in the Lord; wait for Him and patiently lean yourself upon Him; fret not yourself"

Psalm 37:7 AMPC

*I*n the early years of marriage, Alistair and I booked ourselves what we thought would be a relaxing holiday in the sun. Shortly after arriving at the hotel, we were welcomed by an over-enthusiastic and animated holiday rep who easily convinced us to register for all the free sports available throughout our stay. Pistol-shooting, quoits, French boules, water aerobics, archery and other exertions ensured the week flew by. Little did we know on sign-up that only a few other holidaymakers engaged in these sports and those who participated were of Olympian gait, very skilled and competitive, especially when it came to archery. Let's just say the archery experience lingers in my memory and it really didn't help that my sunglasses were smeared with sunscreen lotion. I now have a fresh appreciation for those of the tribe of Benjamin every time I read of them, "All of them were expert archers, and they could shoot arrows or sling stones with their left hand as well as their right."[219]

I came across an interesting Greek word with archery associations. I was studying the subject of "rest" when I lighted upon the word "anesis". Paul used it when writing to the believers in the city of Thessalonica who were undergoing stress and pressure amid a climate of persecution. He said, "And God will provide rest for you who are being persecuted".[220] The word "anesis", translated as "rest", means to let up, to relax, to stop being stressed, or to find relief. An interesting fact I discovered was that it was used in the secular Greek world to

---

[219] 1 Chronicles 12:2 NLT
[220] 2 Thessalonians 1:7 NLT

denote the release of a bowstring that has been under great pressure. Isn't that a beautiful picture of release and relief? Life has a way of becoming stressful if left unmanaged. Like a pulled back bowstring, we need the reminder to rest and stress less. The Psalmist shared his personal experience, "Out of my distress I called on the Lord; the Lord answered me and set me free."[221]

Continuing on the trail of "rest" I discovered another Greek word for it, used by Jesus: "I will give you rest"[222] and "You will find rest for your souls."[223] The word He chose, "anapausis" means to give rest, refresh, to have a purposeful pause. The seas ebb and flow, the moon waxes and wanes, the sun rises and sets with purposeful rhythm. In similar manner Jesus wanted his disciples to punctuate times of intense productivity with times of pause, rest and refreshment. Even music itself has a symbol called a rest, reminding the player of necessary intervals of silence. In a culture that wears busyness as a badge of honour, we should listen to the voice of our wonderful Counsellor saying, "Come to me, all you who are weary and burdened, and I will give you rest."[224] As David phrased it, "Be still and rest in the Lord; wait for Him and patiently lean yourself upon Him; fret not yourself".[225]

Don't be a victim of fruitless fretting. An unknown author aptly penned:

We mutter and sputter, we fume and we spurt;
We mumble and grumble, our feelings get hurt;
We can't understand things, our vision grows dim,
When all that we need is communion with Him!

[221] Psalm 118:5 ESV
[222] Matthew 11:28 NKJV
[223] Matthew 11:29 NKJV
[224] Matthew 11:29 NIV
[225] Psalm 37:7 AMPC

34

WHAT I HAVE WRITTEN, I HAVE WRITTEN

"Now it was the Preparation Day of the Passover, and about the sixth hour. And he said to the Jews, 'Behold your King!'"
John 19:14 NKJV

*I*t appears that we associate certain colours with particular brands. For example, mention red and you might think of Coca-Cola or Vodaphone. Orange might remind you to book a flight with easyJet or slip out to Sainsbury's for that missing ingredient. Allude to green and you might envisage Starbucks, Aer Lingus or possibly John Deere tractors. Blue might conjure up thoughts of Tesco, Facebook or banking institutions such as Barclays. Speak of the colour purple and you probably are thinking of a chocolate brand. Its most recognisable long-standing association is with Cadbury chocolate. But the distinctive purple is also used by rival manufacturer Nestlé for its hazelnut and caramel chocolate called the Purple One and the Quality Street box decoration. The Cadbury brothers picked the colour as a tribute to Queen Victoria.

Purple has been associated with royalty and power for centuries. Queen Elizabeth I forbade anyone but close relatives of the royal family to wear purple. Purple's elite status emanates from the rarity of the dye originally used to produce it. Fabric traders harvested the dye from mucus secreted by the marine murex snail that was only found in the Tyre region of the Mediterranean Sea. A lot of work went into producing the dye, as apparently more than 9,000 mollusks were needed to create just one gram of Tyrian purple. Clothes made from the dye were therefore exorbitantly expensive and linked to royalty.

On the night of His trial prior to the crucifixion, Jesus was mocked as a king. They placed a crown of thorns on His head and clothed Him in raiment of purple to depict royalty. Mark tells us, "Then the soldiers led Him away into the hall called Praetorium, and they called together the whole garrison. And they clothed Him with purple; and they twisted a crown of thorns, put it on His head, and began to salute Him, 'Hail, King of the Jews!' Then they struck Him on the head with a reed and spat on Him; and bowing the knee, they worshiped Him. And when they had mocked Him, they took the purple off Him, put His own clothes on Him, and led Him out to crucify Him."[226]

Later, Pilate had an inscription prepared and fastened to the cross. It read, "Jesus of Nazareth, the King of the Jews."[227] This caused a furore among the Jews who said to Pilate, "Do not write, 'The King of the Jews' but rather, 'This man said, I am King of the Jews.' Pilate answered, 'What I have written I have written.'."[228] Jesus was and is indeed the King of kings and Lord of lords, "the blessed and only Potentate, the King of kings and Lord of lords".[229] He shall reign forevermore and at the name of Jesus every knee will bow. He is "far above all principality and power and might and dominion, and every name that is named, not only in this age but also in that which is to come".[230] May we seek first His kingdom and live to serve His majesty.

---

[226] Mark 15:16–20 NKJV
[227] John 19:19 ESV
[228] John 19:21–22 ESV
[229] 1 Timothy 6:15 NKJV
[230] Ephesians 121 NKJV

35

FTDCRW

"Fret not thyself"

Psalm 37:1 KJV

TDCRW. No, I haven't nodded off at the computer and hit random letters, even though they are all found on the same part of the keyboard! These letters have meaning and are inscribed in the margin of my Bible beside the first seven verses of Psalm 37. Let me share:

Verse 1 says, "Fret not thyself because of evildoers". Fret not. Three times it says "Fret not" in Psalm 37. Sometimes we need to hear something once and we've got it. Sometimes we need to hear it twice and then we get it. Sometimes we need to hear it the third time before we get it. Fret not. Fret not. Fret not!

Fretting is to allow anxiety to run amok, to distress yourself, to get bothered. Remember Jesus said, "Martha, Martha, you are worried and bothered and anxious about so many things."[231] You might hear a person referred to as being het up. "He's het up over something." That's short for "heated up" and conveys the idea of the Hebrew word behind "fret". Again, back to Martha, "Master, don't you care that my sister has abandoned the kitchen to me? Tell her to lend me a hand." The Master said, "Martha, dear Martha, you're fussing far too much and getting yourself worked up over nothing."[232]

What brings down the fever of fretting? The answer is found in verse 3, "Trust in the Lord". Or "Trust (lean on, rely on, and be confident) in the Lord and do good; so shall you dwell in the land and feed surely on His faithfulness, and truly you shall be fed."[233] Rather than feeding on

---

[231] Luke 10:41 AMP
[232] Luke 10:40 MSG
[233] Psalm 37:3 AMPC

the newsfeed and whatever is trending, we are to "feed on His faithfulness" and His truth. The Proverb says, "Trust in the Lord with all your heart and lean not on your own understanding."[234] To "lean not on your own understanding" is to lean completely into the strong arms of God's holding. It means not relying on ourselves, essentially letting go of what we think we know and letting God take the helm of what He perfectly knows.

Then, verse 4 states, "Delight thyself also in the Lord: and he shall give thee the desires of thine heart." When you delight in someone you want to be as close to them as possible. You want to be in their presence. You want to hear their voice and you hang on their every word. This is evident in David's life: "As a deer pants for flowing streams, so pants my soul for you, O God".[235] "A single day in your courts is better than a thousand anywhere else!"[236]

Verse 5 tells us, "Commit thy way unto the Lord; trust also in him; and he shall bring it to pass." "Commit" is from the Hebrew word "gadal" meaning to roll, as of stones. The Amplified Bible brings this out: "Commit your way to the Lord [roll and repose each care of your load on Him]; trust (lean on, rely on, and be confident) also in Him and He will bring it to pass."

Then, "Rest in the Lord" (verse 7). Or, "Be still and rest in the Lord."[237] Let be. Cease striving. Fret not. Learn to rest in the Lord. In the words of another Psalm, "Surrender your anxiety! Be silent and stop your striving and you will see that I am God. I am the God above all the nations, and I will be exalted throughout the whole earth."[238]

Finally, "and wait patiently for him". I love the words, "Wait and hope for and expect the Lord; be brave and of good courage and let your heart be stout and enduring. Yes, wait for and hope for and expect the Lord."[239] God's timing is perfect. In the meantime, be of good courage. Wait for and hope for and expect the Lord.

---

[234] Proverb 3:5 NKJV

[235] Psalm 42:1 ESV

[236] Psalm 84:10 ESV

[237] Psalm 37:7 AMPC

[238] Psalm 46:10 TPT

[239] Psalm 27:14 AMPC

FTDCRW – Fret not … Trust in the Lord … Delight yourself in the Lord … Commit your way to the Lord … Rest in Him … Wait patiently for Him.

36

WHAT'S DOWN IN THE WELL COMES UP WITH THE BUCKET

"Keep thy heart with all diligence"

Proverbs 4:23 KJV

Our children used to play with a plush purple dinosaur who loved to sing when his paw was pressed. One of his iconic songs was "Head, Shoulders, Knees and Toes, Knees and Toes. Head, Shoulders, Knees and Toes, Knees and Toes. And Eyes and Ears and Mouth and Nose. Head, Shoulders, Knees and Toes". Today's focus is also on anatomy: ears, eyes, heart, mouth and feet. Proverbs 4 tells us, "My son, attend to my words; incline thine ear unto my sayings. Let them not depart from thine eyes; keep them in the midst of thine heart. For they are life unto those that find them, and health to all their flesh. Keep thy heart with all diligence; for out of it are the issues of life. Put away from thee a froward mouth, and perverse lips put far from thee. Let thine eyes look right on, and let thine eyelids look straight before thee. Ponder the path of thy feet, and let all thy ways be established. Turn not to the right hand nor to the left: remove thy foot from evil."[240]

Incline your ear to God's Word. The word "attend" in verse 20 means to give your undivided attention. Tune in to what God is saying. Listen diligently. The Bible states, "But this is what I commanded them, saying, 'Obey My voice, and I will be your God, and you shall be My people. And walk in all the ways that I have commanded you, that it may be well with you.' Yet they did not obey or incline their ear, but followed the counsels and the dictates of their evil hearts, and went backward and not forward."[241] May it be well with us as we incline our ears.

---

[240] Proverbs 4:20–27 KJV
[241] Jeremiah 7:23–24 NKJV

Fix your eyes on the Truth. "Let them not depart from thine eyes."[242] The Hebrew brings out the idea of never losing view of His words. Keep them in plain view at all times. Learn them by heart so that you can apply them to every situation. Remember "they are life unto those that find them, and health to all their flesh".[243] Paul stated, "For whatever things were written before were written for our learning, that we through the patience and comfort of the Scriptures might have hope."[244]

Remember to "keep thy heart with all diligence; for out of it are the issues of life".[245] The word translated as "keep" means to guard, protect, or watch over. It assumes that what is to be kept will be under attack, and that the keeper should be sufficiently aware of the attacks so that he will be vigilantly on guard. We know how important the heart is, "For as he thinks in his heart, so is he."[246]

Watch your mouth. "Put away from thee a froward mouth".[247] A guarded heart results in a guarded mouth. Jesus said, "For out of the abundance of the heart the mouth speaks."[248] As the saying goes, "What's down in the well comes up in the bucket!"

Finally, "Ponder the path of your feet." The Passion Translation tells us, "Watch where you're going! Stick to the path of truth, and the road will be safe and smooth before you. Don't allow yourself to be sidetracked for even a moment or take the detour that leads to darkness."[249]

Ears, eyes, heart, mouth and feet – incline your ear to His words; fix your eyes on the Truth; keep your heart diligently; watch what comes from your mouth and ponder the path of your feet.

---

[242] Proverbs 4:21 KJV
[243] Proverbs 4:22 KJV
[244] Romans 15:4 NKJV
[245] Proverbs 4:23 KJV
[246] Proverbs 23:7 NKJV
[247] Proverbs 4:24 KJV
[248] Matthew 12:34 NKJV
[249] Proverbs 4:26–27 TPT

37

SIDE BY SIDE

"But whatever happens to me, remember always to live as Christians should, so that whether I ever see you again or not, I will keep on hearing good reports that you are standing side by side with one strong purpose – to tell the Good News."

Philippians 1:27 TLB

As believers we are to stand side by side with one strong purpose. Someone who stood side by side with Paul was Epaphroditus, mentioned in Philippians, "I have thought it necessary to send to you Epaphroditus my brother and fellow worker and fellow soldier, and your messenger and minister to my need."[250] Pay particular attention to the fivefold description of him:

– *brother*. Above all else he calls him a brother. They had both placed their faith in the Lord Jesus Christ and in His finished work on the cross on their behalf. And thus, they had a precious bond. Above all else we too are brothers and sisters in Christ. We are to love as brothers. "Finally, all of you be of one mind, having compassion for one another; love as brothers, be tenderhearted, be courteous"[251] and "Keep on loving each other as brothers and sisters."[252] Paul told us, "Be devoted to one another in brotherly love; give preference to one another in honor."[253]

– *fellow worker*. The Greek word "sunergos" for "fellow worker" refers to someone who is a team player. It conveys the idea of an affectionate partnership. The Bible reminds us, "For we are fellow workmen (joint promoters, laborers together) with and for God".[254] The word "sunergos" is where we get our English word "synergy". Synergy

---

[250] Philippians 2:25 ESV
[251] 1 Peter 3:8 NKJV
[252] Hebrews 13:1 NIV
[253] Romans 12:10 NASB
[254] 1 Corinthians 3:9 AMPC

is defined as "The interaction or cooperation of two or more organizations, substances, or other agents to produce a combined effect greater than the sum of their separate effects".[255]

– *Fellow soldier.* This pictures saints fighting side by side against an onslaught from seen and unseen foes. J.B. Phillips connects with this picture, translating it as "comrade-in-arms".

– *Messenger.* This conveys the basic idea of one who is sent to do an assignment. We are emissaries of the Lord, envoys, ambassadors with the glorious Gospel to proclaim.

– *Minister.* The Greek word used here is "leitourgos". In ancient Greece, "leitourgoi" were people who, because they loved their city so much, at their own expense undertook certain duties. It might have been to meet the cost of putting on a drama, or paying for the training of athletes who would represent their city in the games, or of equipping a warship and paying for a crew to serve aboard. The example of Epaphroditus shows us one who selflessly served and ministered to the needs of others, including Paul.

Let us value one another as brothers and sisters in Christ who belong to the same family; as fellow workers who labour for the same cause and purpose; as fellow soldiers who share the same trials as comrades in arms; as messengers who live to further the same Gospel and as ministers who have the same compassion to help those in need.

---

[255] Lexico.com

38

BACKSTAGE PREPARATION TO ONSTAGE PRESENTATION

"So Samuel took the horn of oil and anointed him in the presence of his brothers, and from that day on the Spirit of the Lord came powerfully upon David"

1 Samuel 16:13 NIV

*G*od works backstage in our lives. I checked the meaning of "backstage" in *Merriam-Webster*: "Of, relating to, or occurring in the area behind the stage and especially in the dressing rooms; of or relating to the private lives of theater people; of or relating to the inner working or operation (as of an organization)."[256]

If we consider the account in the Bible about David, his backstory as a shepherd was the backstage preparation for his ultimate onstage presentation as shepherd and leader of Israel. Where was David when Samuel came to Jesse's house to anoint David as king? We read, "Jesse made seven of his sons pass before Samuel. And Samuel said to Jesse, 'The Lord has not chosen these.' And Samuel said to Jesse, 'Are all the young men here?' Then he said, 'There remains yet the youngest, and there he is, keeping the sheep.'."[257]

He was out in the fields watching sheep. This was his backstage preparation ground for a showdown with Goliath. When he stepped forward to face Goliath, Saul protested, but David said to Saul, "Your servant used to keep his father's sheep, and when a lion or a bear came and took a lamb out of the flock, I went out after it and struck it, and delivered the lamb from its mouth; and when it arose against me, I caught it by its beard, and struck and killed it. Your servant has killed

---

[256] Merriam-Webster. com
[257] 1 Samuel 16:10–11 NKJV

both lion and bear; and this uncircumcised Philistine will be like one of them, seeing he has defied the armies of the living God."[258]

Be careful not to despise small beginnings. Rather appreciate that God has set you where you are right now for such a time as this. Appreciate your backstage now because it is preparation for your ultimate onstage destiny where God is leading you. God has his stage crew getting in place for the next scene in your life. Stick with His script and rely on the promptings of the Holy Spirit. Remember that backstage is the place where you find the dressing room. This is where your character is cast and cultivated. Here's sound advice: "So, chosen by God for this new life of love, dress in the wardrobe God picked out for you: compassion, kindness, humility, quiet strength, discipline. Be even-tempered, content with second place, quick to forgive an offense. Forgive as quickly and completely as the Master forgave you. And regardless of what else you put on, wear love. It's your basic, all-purpose garment. Never be without it."[259]

Backstage we are prepared and clad for our calling and purpose.

It was written of David's leadership later in life, "And David shepherded them with integrity of heart; with skillful hands he led them."[260] Something interesting I noticed when David had arrived at the scene of Goliath was that his oldest brother Eliab said to him, "Why did you come down here? And with whom have you left those few sheep in the wilderness?"[261] Or, as another translation puts it, "Why aren't you minding your own business, tending that scrawny flock of sheep?"[262] His words were belittling but David did not allow them to affect his destiny. Others may not appreciate the season you are in, but stay faithful and allow God to hone you for His intentional purposes.

---

[258] 1 Samuel 17:34–36 NKJV
[259] Colossians 3:12–14 MSG
[260] Psalm 78:72 NIV
[261] 1 Samuel 17:28 NKJV
[262] 1 Samuel 17:28 MSG

39

THE POTENTIAL IS EXPONENTIAL!

"Again he said, 'What shall we say the kingdom of God is like, or what parable shall we use to describe it?'"

Mark 4:30 NIV

*I*n Mark 4 the mustard seed is Jesus' preferred reference for all things small. It furnished Him with a visual example, "What shall we say the kingdom of God is like, or what parable shall we use to describe it? It is like a mustard seed, which is the smallest of all seeds on earth. Yet when planted, it grows and becomes the largest of all garden plants, with such big branches that the birds can perch in its shade."[263]

Jesus likened the kingdom of God to a grain of mustard seed, whose small initial form contrasted with its impressive final form of "such big branches" and exponential growth. In Genesis God speaks to Abraham, "I will make you into a great nation."[264] Then He goes exponential and declares that Abraham is going to be "a father of many nations".[265] He continues, "I will make you exceedingly fruitful; and I will make nations of you, and kings shall come from you."[266] Exponential increase indeed! However, Abraham's perspective was limited. God took him outside of his tent to see beyond the confines of its curtains. "'Look now toward heaven, and count the stars if you are able to number them.' And He said to him, 'So shall your descendants be.'."[267] Taking Him outside was His way of telling Abraham not to put ceilings on what He wanted to do through him. We are very similar to Abraham. God wants to get us outside of our limited perspective, beyond the bounds of human

---

[263] Mark 4:30–32 NIV
[264] Genesis 12:2 NIV
[265] Genesis 17:5 NKJV
[266] Genesis 17:6 NKJV
[267] Genesis 15:5 NKJV

brainstorming, to see the magnitude of His desire for us. Abraham was thinking addition. God was thinking multiplication. Abraham was thinking a son. God was thinking a nation, and many nations beyond that. God goes for the exponential. Let's not ask God for what we see as possible. Let's ask Him for what we see as impossible. Let's not pray based on our limitations. Let us pray based on God's exponential possibilities.

Ephesians 3:20 reminds us to ask for "infinitely more". Paul wrote, "Now all glory to God, who is able, through his mighty power at work within us, to accomplish infinitely more than we might ask or think."[268] Or, in another translation, "Now to Him who is able to do exceedingly abundantly above all that we ask or think".[269] Jesus told us the potential is exponential, "But you shall receive power when the Holy Spirit has come upon you; and you shall be witnesses to Me in Jerusalem, and in all Judea and Samaria, and to the end of the earth."[270] "To the ends of the earth" evangelism is the plan. As Jesus said, "Go into all the world and preach the gospel to every creature."[271]

What tents are blocking your vision today and causing you to settle for less? What self-made restrictions are hindering you from seeing the grand design of God's will and the expansion of His kingdom? Hear the invitation of God to step out of your tent. Allow God's Word to embed "exponential" into your perception.

---

[268] Ephesians 3:20 NLT
[269] Ephesians 3:20 NKJV
[270] Acts 1:8 NKJV
[271] Mark 16:15 NKJV

40

ORDINARY VESSELS

"He shall be a vessel unto honour, sanctified, and meet for the master's use, and prepared unto every good work."

2 Timothy 2:21 KJV

I remember visiting antique shops as a child. Each visit was accompanied with a stern warning attached before entering – Do not touch anything! There was plenty of temptation as the shops were usually cramped and crammed with a collection of artefacts ranging from wooden butter boxes and crates, whiskey barrels, terracotta jars, handwoven baskets, basic bowls, vintage vases, jugs, pots and pans, vials, crystal goblets, porcelain dishes, all products of a bygone era. What I did recall was this – the essential, everyday run-of-the-mill objects were usually placed at ground level or eye level, but the expensive decorative vases were top shelf. The higher up you looked, the more ornamental or nonfunctional the object appeared to be.

This memory flooded back to me while reading 2 Timothy 2:21, our verse today. "He shall be a vessel unto honour, sanctified, and meet for the master's use, and prepared unto every good work." We are God's vessels. The Greek word is "skeuos" which refers to a vessel, a receptacle, a functional container or utensil. The Lord said to Ananias regarding Paul, "He is a chosen vessel unto me, to bear my name before the Gentiles, and kings, and the children of Israel."[272]

But we also are chosen vessels unto God, to bear His name before the people of our generation. Paul tells us, "But we have this treasure in earthen vessels, that the excellency of the power may be of God, and not of us."[273] We are earthen vessels. Or, "We are like common clay jars that carry this glorious treasure within, so that the extraordinary

---

[272] Acts 9:15 KJV
[273] 2 Corinthians 4:7 KJV

overflow of power will be seen as God's, not ours." [274] Ordinary terracotta containers. But we carry glorious measure within.

God showed me something amazing in His Word. He showed me how it was the ordinary everyday vessels in the Bible that witnessed the miracles! The baskets, the waterpots, the barrels and jars and cooking pans. The baskets bore testimony of a mighty miracle where Jesus took the five small loaves and the two fish and miraculously fed a multitude. We read, "And everyone ate until they were satisfied, for the food was multiplied in front of their eyes! They picked up the leftovers and filled up twelve baskets full!"[275] What a miracle!

Then there were the stoneware waterpots. The setting was a wedding celebration in Cana of Galilee recorded in John 2. These waterpots witnessed what was called the first sign of Jesus, as He turned water into wine. We are told, "This miraculous sign at Cana in Galilee was the first time Jesus revealed his glory."[276]

The barrel and cruse or jug also were instrumental in a miracle concerning Elijah and the widow at Zarephath. We read, "For thus saith the Lord God of Israel, 'The barrel of meal shall not waste, neither shall the cruse of oil fail, until the day that the Lord sendeth rain upon the earth.'."[277] Empty jars were used by his successor Elisha and a widow, jars that miraculously kept filling with oil. Then there was the cooking pan that got to cook the heavenly manna, the bread of angels! [278] Ordinary vessels that were used in extraordinary ways to show forth the glory of God. Remember, "We carry this precious Message around in the unadorned clay pots of our ordinary lives. That's to prevent anyone from confusing God's incomparable power with us."[279]

---

[274] 2 Corinthians 4:7 TPT
[275] Matthew 14:20 TPT
[276] John 2:11 NLT
[277] 1 Kings 17:14 KJV
[278] Numbers 11:7–9
[279] 2 Corinthians 4:7 MSG

41

ARE YOU PUZZLED?

"He is never puzzled over what to do!"

Isaiah 40:28 TPT

Are you someone who enjoys a puzzle and seeks to stimulate your cognitive function on a daily basis? I'm told that the two hemispheres of the brain control different functions. The left side controls analytic and logical thinking and the right side controls creativity. Puzzles activate both the left and right hemispheres of the brain, giving you a real mental workout. I must admit that I prefer puzzles that focus on words, rather than numbers, shapes or logic. Hence, I often skip the sudoku in favour of a good old cryptic crossword. I gravitate toward the online scrabble app and word tile games. The word "to puzzle" comes from "pusle" meaning "to bewilder, confound, perplex with difficult problems or questions".[280] Some synonyms of the verb "to puzzle" are befuddle, flummox, perplex and baffle. When Paul was addressing the Corinthian church, he said this, "We are perplexed, but not in despair."[281] Other translations read, "perplexed, but not driven to despair".[282] "We are puzzled, but never in despair".[283] "At times we don't know what to do, but quitting is not an option"[284] and "We're not sure what to do, but we know that God knows what to do."[285]

In his second letter to the church in Corinth, Paul shared a long litany of trials he had experienced while preaching the gospel. Paul was beaten, dragged in and out of prison, persecuted, robbed, flogged excessively

---

[280] www.etymonline.com
[281] 2 Corinthians 4:8 NKJV
[282] 2 Corinthians 4:8 ESV
[283] 2 Corinthians 4:8 JB Phillips translation
[284] 2 Corinthians 4:8 TPT
[285] 2 Corinthians 4:8 MSG

and pelted with stones. He faced shipwrecks, angry mobs, sleepless nights, hunger and thirst – and received thirty-nine lashes on five different occasions. He had been at death's door time after time.[286] Because Paul maintained a Christ-centred perspective in times of adversity, he could say, "We are hard-pressed on every side, yet not crushed; we are perplexed, but not in despair; persecuted, but not forsaken; struck down, but not destroyed."[287]

Notice for every negative experience Paul experienced, he highlighted the positive. Yes, he was hard-pressed, perplexed, persecuted and struck down. But in Paul's mind, he was not crushed, in despair, not forsaken by God or destroyed. *Strong's Lexicon* tells us that the word translated as "perplexed" is "aporeo", meaning "to be without resources, to be in straits, to be left wanting, to be embarrassed, to be in doubt, not to know which way to turn". It literally means to be without a way or path. To be "in despair" is "exaporeo", an intensified form meaning to be utterly at loss, be utterly destitute of measures or resources, to renounce all hope. But Paul says we are not in despair. We are not without hope. The God of hope fills us with all joy and peace in believing. We know that God is still at work. We are not without help. Isaiah tells us concerning God, "Don't you know? Haven't you been listening? Yahweh is the one and only everlasting God, the Creator of all you can see and imagine! He never gets weary or worn out. His intelligence is unlimited; he is never puzzled over what to do!"[288] I love those words, "he is never puzzled over what to do!" Therefore, trust Him. Don't be driven to despair. No matter how difficult the terrain, highlight the positive and hone in on His purpose.

---

[286] 2 Corinthians 11:23–27
[287] 2 Corinthians 4:8–9 NKJV
[288] Isaiah 40:28 TPT

42

ARE YOU POLISHING YOUR CHARIOT AND GROOMING YOUR HORSE?

"Some trust in chariots, and some in horses: but we will remember the name of the Lord our God."

Psalm 20:7 KJV

I was reading through Psalm 20 when verse 7 caught my attention. It states, "Some trust in chariots, and some in horses: but we will remember the name of the Lord our God."[289] Contrasts can bring out the truth more vividly and this is a classic example. Of great significance here is the Hebrew word for "remember", "zakar", meaning "to call to mind, recall, bring to remembrance". David was a valiant warrior, but he remembered and placed his confidence in the name of the Lord. Another translation reads, "Some find their strength in their weapons and wisdom, but my miracle deliverance can never be won by men. Our boast is in the Lord our God, who makes us strong and gives us victory!"[290]

Remember where your victory comes from. Remember the name of the Lord our God. Call to mind the comprehensive character of God expressed in His covenantal faithfulness. It was this attitude that fortified the youthful David in his victorious combat with Goliath. He said to the Philistine, "You come to me with a sword, with a spear, and with a javelin. But I come to you in the name of the Lord of hosts, the God of the armies of Israel, whom you have defied."[291]

Remember His Name. Concerning the name of the Lord, David not only praised His name (Psalm 7:17), called upon His name (Psalm 116:17), and proclaimed the excellence of His name (Psalm 8:1), but he

---

[289] Psalm 20:7 KJV
[290] Psalm 20:7 TPT
[291] 1 Samuel 17:45 NKJV

also wrote these words: "We will remember the name of the Lord our God." He said, "Those who know your name trust in you, for you, Lord, have never forsaken those who seek you"[292] and "Our help is in the name of the Lord, who made heaven and earth."[293]

Some trust in chariots said David. In David's day chariots were a mark of great military strength. They were fierce and intimidating. Razor-sharp blades were fastened to their undercarriage and sometimes extended from each wheel as far as nine feet so that they could mow the enemy down like grass. Some trust in horses, said David. In the ancient world, the horse was a symbol of authority and power. But David was banking on God's reputation and encourages us to do the same. Are you willing to ask the hard question: What are the "chariots and horses" you have been relying on? Will you shun your favourite props and most cherished substitutes and be weaned from other dependencies? Jeremiah said, "Thus says the Lord: 'Let not the wise man glory in his wisdom, let not the mighty man glory in his might, nor let the rich man glory in his riches; but let him who glories glory in this, that he understands and knows Me'."[294] Our boast is not in the brains, bling or brawn of man but we confide in the calibre of our God. "The name of the Lord is a strong tower: the righteous run into it, and are safe."[295] Some may trust in chariots and horses, the appendages of war. But we will do differently. We will remember the name of the Lord our God. In a modern translation, "See those people polishing their chariots, and those others grooming their horses? But we're making garlands for God our God. The chariots will rust, those horses pull up lame – and we'll be on our feet, standing tall."[296]

---

[292] Psalm 9:10 NIV
[293] Psalm 124:8 NKJV
[294] Jeremiah 9:23–24 NKJV
[295] Proverbs 18:10 NKJV
[296] Psalm 20:7 MSG

43

SPEAK BY THE SPIRIT

"For the Holy Spirit will teach you in that very hour what you ought to say."

Luke 12:12 NKJV

Today he is referred to as Peter the Great and his throne is on display in the Armoury Chamber in Moscow. Peter first came to the throne in 1682 as a ten-year-old co-Tsar with his older half-brother Ivan V who was in poor health. For a short time both brothers jointly ruled Russia, seated on a double-seated throne. Peter's older half-sister Sophia transmitted relevant information to them through a small orifice cut into the back of the throne and concealed by a velvet covering. She would listen into their meetings with dignitaries and whisper back information and responses they were to repeat verbatim. This way they appeared sagacious and informed.

This reminds me of what Jesus told us, "The Holy Spirit will give you the words to say at the moment when you need them."[297] Or, in another translation, "Simply be confident and allow the Spirit of Wisdom access to your heart, and he will reveal in that very moment what you are to say to them."[298]

We have the Spirit of Wisdom to prompt us and give us the right words for every occasion. Speaking of the Holy Spirit, Jesus said, "And I will ask the Father, and He will give you another Comforter (Counselor, Helper, Intercessor, Advocate, Strengthener, and Standby), that He may remain with you forever."[299] Let us appreciate afresh the 24/7 ministry of the Holy Spirit. In the same chapter Jesus taught, "But the Helper, the Holy Spirit, whom the Father will send in My name, He

---

[297] Luke 12:12 The Voice
[298] Luke 12:12 TPT
[299] John 14:16 AMPC

will teach you all things, and bring to your remembrance all things that I said to you."[300]

I have lost track of how many times the Holy Spirit has brought a verse for me to share, exactly relevant for the situation. The Bible says, "Simply speak with the words of wisdom that I will give you that moment, and none of your persecutors will be able to withstand the grace and wisdom that comes from your mouths."[301] Seven men of good reputation, full of the Holy Spirit and of wisdom, were appointed as deacons, one of whom was Stephen. When opponents confronted and disputed with Stephen it was reported, "None of them could stand against the wisdom and the Spirit with which Stephen spoke."[302] God said to Moses, "Now therefore, go, and I will be with your mouth and teach you what you shall say."[303] He said to Jeremiah, "And whatever I command you, you shall speak. Do not be afraid of their faces, for I am with you to deliver you," says the Lord. Then the Lord put forth His hand and touched my mouth, and the Lord said to me: 'Behold, I have put My words in your mouth.'."[304] David stated, "The Spirit of the Lord spoke by me, and His word was on my tongue."[305] Paul requested of the Ephesians, "Pray also for me, that whenever I speak, words may be given me so that I will fearlessly make known the mystery of the gospel."[306] May we speak what the Spirit reveals.

---

[300] John 14:26 NKJV
[301] Luke 21:15 TPT
[302] Acts 6:10 NLT
[303] Exodus 4:12 NKJV
[304] Jeremiah 1:8–9 NKJV
[305] 2 Samuel 23:2 NKJV
[306] Ephesians 6:19 NIV

44

HOW DEEPLY INTIMATE

"I have been crucified with Christ; it is no longer I who live, but Christ lives in me; and the life which I now live in the flesh I live by faith in the Son of God, who loved me and gave Himself for me."

Galatians 2:20 NKJV

The story is told of a five-year-old boy whose sister was suffering from a rare disease. Her only chance of recovery appeared to be a blood transfusion from her brother. He was the perfect candidate because he had the same blood type and had miraculously survived the same condition himself. When the doctor explained the situation and asked the boy if he would be willing to give his blood to his sister, he initially hesitated but only for a moment. Taking a deep breath, he agreed. As the transfusion progressed, he lay in bed next to his sister and smiled, seeing the colour returning to her cheeks. Then his own face grew pale and his smile faded. He looked up at the doctor and asked with a trembling voice, "Will I start dying right away?" The little boy had misunderstood the doctor. He had thought that with his blood donation, he would be literally giving his life to save his sister's.

As remarkable as that story is, another is even more riveting. Paul captured it in his letter to the Romans, "But God demonstrates his own love for us in this: While we were still sinners, Christ died for us."[307] May we have a fresh revelation of such redemptive love, a love that is given even if it's not received or returned! The Bible says, "By this we

---

[307] Romans 5:8 NIV

know love, because He laid down His life for us".[308] Paul testified about "the Son of God, who loved me and gave Himself for me".[309]

If by grace you have placed your faith in Jesus Christ and His finished work, these words are not merely letters upon a page. These words are your testimony. Not only do I know that Jesus Christ loved Paul, but He loved me. He shed His precious blood for me. This is so deeply intimate and personal. He loved me and gave Himself for me. True, we read and believe that "God so loved the world, that he gave his only begotten Son, that whosoever believeth in him should not perish, but have everlasting life."[310] Yes, you and I are a "whosoever". But isn't it wonderful to say, He loved me and gave Himself for me?

John invites us to see this great love for ourselves, "See what great love the Father has lavished on us, that we should be called children of God! And that is what we are!"[311] Paul prays, "And may you have the power to understand, as all God's people should, how wide, how long, how high, and how deep his love is. May you experience the love of Christ, though it is too great to understand fully. Then you will be made complete with all the fullness of life and power that comes from God."[312] In the wording of another translation I invite you to experience, "the great magnitude of the astonishing love of Christ in all its dimensions. How deeply intimate and far-reaching is his love! How enduring and inclusive it is! Endless love beyond measurement that transcends our understanding – this extravagant love pours into you until you are filled to overflowing with the fullness of God!"[313] Go ahead, say it over and over, He loved me and gave Himself for me!

---

[308] 1 John 3:16 NKJV
[309] Galatians 2:20 NKJV
[310] John 3:16 KJV
[311] 1 John 3:1 NIV
[312] Ephesians 3:18–19 NLT
[313] Ephesians 3:18–19 TPT

45

YOU'RE ON MUTE

"Hear, for I will speak excellent and princely things; and the opening of my lips shall be for right things."

Proverbs 8:6 AMP

"Y ou're on mute. Please unmute." This is an oft-repeated phrase with users of Microsoft Teams, Zoom and their compatriots. In video conferencing I have had to be reminded on multiple occasions to unmute. More lamentable however is the fact that in life I often need the reminder that I am in a muted state when I should be speaking up and speaking out. Now, more than ever, Christians need to speak up. The Bible says, "To everything there is a season, a time for every purpose under heaven … a time to keep silence and a time to speak." [314] A time to speak. May the Holy Spirit give us fresh empowerment to speak forth Kingdom words of truth. Words that edify, exhort and encourage. Words that bring alignment. Words that release truth, light, love, grace, peace, hope and faith. Words that shatter darkness. Words that lift up, cheer up and build up. Words that are spirit and life! Jesus said, "The words that I have spoken to you are spirit and life."[315]

We know from the book of Proverbs that the tongue has the power of "death and life"[316] and "The mouth of the righteous is a well of life."[317] Realising the full impact of this, we ought to articulate life. I love Paul's words, "Let no corrupt word proceed out of your mouth, but what is good for necessary edification, that it may impart grace to the hearers."[318] We should be a wellspring of life-giving words that impart

---

[314] Ecclesiastes 3:1, 7 NKJV
[315] John 6:63 ESV
[316] Proverbs 18:21 NKJV
[317] Proverbs 10:11 NKJV
[318] Ephesians 4:29 NKJV

grace and build up, leaving others in an improved state of well-being. Our words should nourish and cause others to flourish. Other translations render the verse, "Let your words become beautiful gifts that encourage others"[319] and "offer only fresh words that build others up when they need it most".[320]

Paul instructed the Colossians, "Let every word you speak be drenched with grace and tempered with truth and clarity. For then you will be prepared to give a respectful answer to anyone who asks about your faith."[321] Dwell on those words, "drenched with grace", "tempered with truth and clarity" and "a respectful answer". Do you know that your words can actually soothe and heal? Proverbs 12:18 says that "the tongue of the wise promotes health"[322] or "the words of the wise soothe and heal".[323]

Are you promoting health? Are you pouring on the healing balm with your words? Wisdom says, "Hear, for I will speak excellent and princely things; and the opening of my lips shall be for right things."[324]

I declare that the opening of my lips shall be for right things. Right now, the world is full of voices that are causing panic, anxiety, frustration and hopelessness. News. Internet. Politicians. Almost every voice is speaking forth doom and gloom. That is why the world needs to hear from you. Please unmute.

---

[319] Ephesians 4:29 TPT
[320] Ephesians 4:29 The Voice
[321] Colossians 4:6 TPT
[322] Proverbs 12:18 NKJV
[323] Proverbs 12:18 TPT
[324] Proverbs 8:6 AMP

46

A WORTHWHILE QUOTE ON A POST-IT NOTE

"Then Isaac sowed in that land, and reaped in the same year a hundredfold"

Genesis 26:12 NKJV

I want to draw your attention to a quote which God highlighted for me twice in one day. First, I noticed it amid multiple Post-it notes affixed to the back of my larder door. I recognised it was written in my mother's handwriting, something she deemed worthy to transcribe and deposit in my care. By the dilapidated state of the paper and the jadedness of the ink I could tell that it was Blu-tacked to my larder a number of years ago. But God directed my focus to it this week. Having noticed it after breakfast, I resumed reading a book and what was on the page? Yes, the same quote! Allow me to share it with you in the hope that it will inspire you. It was written by Robert Louis Stevenson: "Don't judge each day by the harvest you reap but by the seeds that you plant."[325]

We love to see the benefits of a great harvest, don't we? However, in the pattern of any commendable farmer we must be conscientious about sowing seeds. We must not let circumstances put us off sowing. As the Bible says, "He who observes the wind [and waits for all conditions to be favorable] will not sow, and he who regards the clouds will not reap."[326] What prayers are you sowing this week? What neighbourhood are you circling in prayer, in anticipation of an abundant harvest? In one of His parables, Jesus commissioned us as seed-sowers.[327] Are you sowing the seed of God's Word, watering it and trusting God for the increase? Remember, seeds do not grow sitting in a packet on your shelf.

---

[325] Robert Louis Stevenson goodreads.com
[326] Ecclesiastes 4:11 AMPC
[327] Mark 4:3–14

They must be planted in the proper place. Last year I had great intentions of growing sunflowers, but the stripy seeds are still stashed away in my utility room cupboard. Psalm 126:5–6 reminds us, "They that sow in tears shall reap in joy. He that goeth forth and weepeth, bearing precious seed, shall doubtless come again with rejoicing, bringing his sheaves with him."[328] We bear precious seed. We can be planting and watering seeds that God will grow into tall, towering oaks of righteousness for His glory (Isaiah 61:3b).

I remember one winter my husband came home after tidying up someone's garden. There was excess soil in his trailer and he dumped it in a corner of our garden. We thought nothing more of it until springtime arrived. Then through that mound of soil sprouted beautiful golden daffodils and splashes of Versace purple in the form of crocuses! Paul gave us wise counsel, "And don't allow yourselves to be weary or disheartened in planting good seeds, for the season of reaping the wonderful harvest you've planted is coming!"[329] Or, "In due season we will reap, if we do not give up."[330] The words "due season" are "idios" and "kairos" in Greek. The word "idios" means "its own". The word "kairos" conveys "a set season". Thus, each seed has its own set season – a specific, individual time when it will produce a harvest. Think of it – a seed. Small. Seemingly insignificant. Possibly forgotten. But filled with potential for growth. For greatness. What are you sowing? Let me encourage you with the words, "Then Isaac sowed in that land, and reaped in the same year a hundredfold; and the Lord blessed him."[331]

---

[328] Psalm 126:5–6 KJV
[329] Galatians 6:9 TPT
[330] Galatians 6:9 ESV
[331] Genesis 26:12 NKJV

47

ARE THE DOGS BARKING?

"Be faithful until death, and I will give you the crown of life."
Revelation 2:10 NKJV

ogs don't normally bark at parked cars. While the car is stationary, nothing stirs. But the moment you pull out of the drive, put your foot on the throttle and accelerate, that's when the yapping and chasing begins. Likewise, it's when you move forward and make progress spiritually that the criticising, mocking and persecution begin in a Christian's life. No one cares when you are idle and ineffective. But try to make a difference and walk in the paths of righteousness; it's then that society is bothered and the snarling starts.

We see this in the life of Polycarp, a man discipled by John the apostle, the beloved disciple of Jesus Himself. He was born in AD 70, a native of Smyrna, and holds a special place in church history as being one of the earliest martyrs about whom we have a detailed eyewitness account. Living in an era when challenges to his teachings came from both internal and external forces, he never swayed. He steadfastly stood against all adversities and passed on precious knowledge to those he mentored. He was inflexible in speaking out against error, a stalwart of the faith.

In the Book of Revelation, Christ had warned the church at Smyrna that they were about to face persecution and promised a crown of life to those who were faithful unto death. Polycarp, Bishop of Smyrna, soon had to apply those words to himself as hostile forces called for his death. His companions convinced him to hide in a farmhouse and later to flee to another where the threat to his life was less immediate. While praying, Polycarp had a vision. He had seen his pillow bursting into flames around his head. Polycarp had no question what the vision meant. Turning to those with him he said, "It must be that I shall be burned alive." By torturing two slaves, the authorities learned of Polycarp's whereabouts. They sent men to arrest him. This time Polycarp refused to run. Instead, he ordered food to be set before his captors and requested only for an hour to pray. When they agreed, Polycarp prayed so earnestly that one hour became two, and several of the soldiers regretted their role in the arrest of such a venerable old man. A magistrate ordered Polycarp to renounce Christ and give obedience to Caesar as Lord. Polycarp answered: "Eighty and six years have I served Christ, nor has He ever done me any harm. How, then, could I blaspheme my King who saved me? You threaten the fire that burns for an hour and then is quenched; but you know not of the fire of the judgment to come, and the fire of eternal punishment. Bring what you will."[332] On 23 February, 155, Polycarp died at the stake. According to eyewitnesses, as the flames grew, they did not consume Polycarp as expected. The fire formed a circle around him, but his body did not burn. Since the fire did not have its intended effect on Polycarp's body, an executioner was ordered to stab him to death with a dagger. His blood extinguished the flames and his testimony lives on.

Paul told us, "In fact, everyone who wants to live a godly life in Christ Jesus will be persecuted."[333] The Greek word for persecuted ("dioko") means to be hunted, as a fox is chased and hunted by bloodhounds. Samuel Rutherford stated that "If ye were not strangers here, the dogs of the world would not bark at you" and "They lose nothing who gain Christ."[334] No matter what assails us or how hot the fires of persecution blaze, may we remain unwavering in our commitment to Jesus Christ.

---

[332] Polycarp of Smyrna. Quoted in a letter from the church of Smyrna.
[333] 2 Timothy 3:12 NIV
[334] Samuel Rutherford (1600–1661, Scottish theologian and pastor)

48

PLUS ULTRA

"Celebrate with praises the God and Father of our Lord Jesus Christ, who has shown us his extravagant mercy. For his fountain of mercy has given us a new life – we are reborn to experience a living, energetic hope through the resurrection of Jesus Christ from the dead. We are reborn into a perfect inheritance that can never perish, never be defiled, and never diminish. It is promised and preserved forever in the heavenly realm for you!"
1 Peter 1:3–5 TPT

*I*n a plaza of Valladolid in Spain there stands a monument commemorating the renowned explorer, Christopher Columbus. Its most interesting feature is a statue of a lion destroying the first of three Latin words, "Non Plus Ultra", words which had been Spain's motto for centuries and were minted on their coins. Translated they mean, "No More Beyond".

Let me give you a little backdrop. At one time Spain controlled both sides of the narrowest part of the Strait of Gibraltar. At the narrowing of the two land masses of Africa and Europe, there was a huge marker called the "Pillar of Hercules", and it carried the three-word Latin chiseled into stone: "Non Plus Ultra". These words served as a warning to sailors and navigators to go no further, essentially shutting the door on possibility. The belief that there was nothing more to discover was so prevalent that "Non Plus Ultra" was written on the edges of maps and seen everywhere the Spanish Standard flew.

However, in 1492, the voyage of Columbus changed everything. On 3 August, he set sail from Palos de la Frontera with a crew of eighty-eight on board three ships, the Nina, the Pinta and the Santa Maria. We know that they sailed through unknown waters to discover the Americas. The world was forever changed. Before his voyages, the Spaniards thought they had reached the outer limits of the earth, "No More Beyond". But, back to the statue, the first Latin word is torn away by the lion's paw, making it now read "Plus Ultra". Columbus had proven that there indeed was "more beyond".

Jesus Christ has undeniably shown us that there is much "more beyond". Like the lion on Columbus' monument deleting the first Latin word, the Lion of Judah has erased the fallacious concept that death was the end and there was no more beyond. On Good Friday as God ebonised the sky, shook the earth, shattered rocks, untombed the entombed and tore apart the veil revealing the Holy of Holies, everything changed. Through Christ's death on the cross and His resurrection from the dead, we can say with assurance that there is plus ultra – more beyond! As Billy Graham said, "For the believer there is hope beyond the grave, because Jesus Christ has opened the door to heaven for us by His death and resurrection." Peter celebrated his living hope in the words "Praise be to the God and Father of our Lord Jesus Christ! In his great mercy he has given us new birth into a living hope through the resurrection of Jesus Christ from the dead, and into an inheritance that can never perish, spoil or fade." [335] Theologian, J.I. Packer (1926–2020), sums it up beautifully, "Optimism is a wish without warrant; Christian hope is a certainty, guaranteed by God himself. Optimism reflects ignorance as to whether good things will ever actually come. Christian hope expresses knowledge that every day of his life, and every moment beyond it, the believer can say with truth, on the basis of God's own commitment, that the best is yet to come."[336]

---

[335] Peter 1:3–4 NIV
[336] https://www.goodreads.com/quotes/275720

49

THE ROYAL MINT

*"Take the first fish that comes up, and when you open its mouth
you will find there a shekel."*

Matthew 17:27 AMPC

Coins can tell us so much about a country. But how much do you know about our currency? I have to admit that I didn't even know that The Royal Mint, which mints the different coins for use in the UK, is located close to Cardiff in Wales. Did you know that Sir Isaac Newton, primarily known for discovering gravity, was Master of the Mint from 1699 until his death in 1727? He applied his scientific mind to the task of improving the accuracy and integrity of coins. Are you aware that every year a random selection of UK coins are tested to ensure that they conform to the required standards of diameter, weight and chemical composition? This procedure, which dates back to the twelfth century, is known as the Trial of the Pyx. "Pyx" translates to "box", and refers to the chests in which the coins are placed for presentation to the jury. It's also a little-known fact that the direction of each monarch's effigy faces in the opposite direction to their immediate predecessor. From 1953 to the present day, twenty-three different portraits of Queen Elizabeth II have appeared on UK coins, with four in circulation today. Did you know that the "coppers" in your change, aren't actually made of copper? Since 1992, 1p and 2p coins have been made of steel, with a copper plating. 1p coins are the most produced coins by the Mint. Two 1ps weigh the same as one 2p and two 5ps weigh the same as one 10p! But now I digress!

Today's verse points to the miracle of finding a coin in a fish's mouth. Not surprisingly, only Matthew, a former tax collector, reports it.

"When they arrived in Capernaum, the collectors of the half shekel [the temple tax] went up to Peter and said, 'Does not your Teacher pay the half shekel?' He answered, 'Yes.' And when he came home, Jesus spoke to him [about it] first, saying, 'What do you think, Simon? From whom do earthly rulers collect duties or tribute – from their own sons or from others not of their own family?' And when Peter said, 'From other people not of their own family,' Jesus said to him, 'Then the sons are exempt. However, in order not to give offense and cause them to stumble [that is, to cause them to judge unfavorably and unjustly] go down to the sea and throw in a hook. Take the first fish that comes up, and when you open its mouth you will find there a shekel. Take it and give it to them to pay the temple tax for Me and for yourself.'."[337]

The Temple tax was a half shekel that every Israelite male above twenty years old had to pay. As we read this account, we discover that there are resources we know not of, but God knows where we can locate them. Why didn't He simply put the coin in Peter's hand instead of him having to go and cast a line? It required a step of faith, trust and obedience on Peter's part. When he obeyed he found a coin, the Greek word "stater", a silver coin which was equivalent to one shekel, and therefore was the exact amount needed for two people. The Bible assures us, "And this same God who takes care of me will supply all your needs from his glorious riches, which have been given to us in Christ Jesus."[338]

From His Royal Mint He shall supply all your need. From His riches in glory you are amply supplied – trust Him.

---

[337] Matthew 17:24–27 AMPC
[338] Philippians 4:19 NLT

50

I WILL AWAKEN THE DAWN

"Along the banks of Babylon's rivers we sat as exiles, mourning our captivity, and wept with great love for Zion. Our music and mirth were no longer heard, only sadness. We hung up our harps on the willow trees."

Psalm 137:1–2 TPT

*D*rooping willows, doleful hearts and discarded harps paint the scene. In a mood of dejection and defiance the children of God decided to hang up their instruments of music and worship. Their music and mirth were no longer heard as they mourned their captivity. How about us today? We must not let our present circumstances dictate the output of our praise to God. Are you drooping? He is the Lifter of our heads. The Bible tells us, "But you, O Lord, are a shield about me, my glory, and the lifter of my head."[339] David speaks to himself saying, "Why are you cast down, O my soul, and why are you in turmoil within me?"[340] Then he has a revelation, "Hope in God; for I shall again praise him, my salvation and my God."[340]

Are you doleful? He gives you the mantle of joyous praise for a spirit of heaviness. Let Him gird you with gladness and turn your mourning into dancing. The Psalmist testified, "We may weep through the night, but at daybreak it will turn into shouts of ecstatic joy"[341] and "Then he broke through and transformed all my wailing into a whirling dance of ecstatic praise! He has torn the veil and lifted from me the sad heaviness of mourning. He wrapped me in the glory-garments of gladness."[342]

---

[339] Psalm 3:3 ESV
[340] Psalm 42:5 ESV
[341] Psalm 30:5 TPT
[342] Psalm 30:11 TPT

David prophetically declared, "Awake, lute and harp! I will awaken the dawn."[343] Rabbinic tradition tells us David purposely placed his harp above his bed. The night breeze would begin to act upon the cords, sending forth those dulcet heavenly sounds, reminding him to lend his voice in accompaniment. In Psalm 57:8 he stated, "Arise, my soul, and sing his praises! My worship will awaken the dawn, greeting the daybreak with my songs of praise!"[344] The song that awakens the dawn is the song that's sung while it is still dark! When Paul and Silas lay in the darkest innermost part of the prison, beaten and bloodied and bound, their fellow prisoners heard them singing in the middle of the night.[345] Habakkuk chose to praise over pain as well," Though the fig tree does not blossom and there is no fruit on the vines ... Yet I will [choose to] rejoice in the Lord; I will [choose to] shout in exultation in the [victorious] God of my salvation!"[346]

It may look dark outside but daybreak is coming. Awaken the dawn with your praise. Don't wait until your environment is conducive to worship. In Psalm 137:4 I noticed something of interest in verse 4. They asked, "How shall we sing the Lord's song in a foreign land?" Notice it is called "the Lord's song". Don't deprive the Lord of His song. Let me encourage you, "Sing to the Lord a new song, and His praise from the end of the earth! You who go down to the sea, and all that is in it, the islands and coastal regions and the inhabitants of them [sing a song such as has never been heard in the heathen world]!"[347]

---

[343] Psalm 108:2 NJKV
[344] Psalm 57:8 TPT
[345] Acts 16:25
[346] Habakkuk 3:17–18 AMP
[347] Isaiah 42:10 AMPC

51

WEAR A SMILE

"A glad heart makes a cheerful face, but by sorrow of heart the spirit is crushed."

Proverbs 15:13 ESV

The title of a song from the Broadway musical *Annie*, written by Charles Strouse and Martin Charnin, provides the keynote of today's devotion: "You're Never Fully Dressed Without a Smile". A.A. Milne, best known for his books about the teddy bear Winnie-the-Pooh, said, "Always wear a smile, because your smile is a reason for many others to smile!"[348] The Bible tells us, "A glad heart makes a cheerful face."[349] Or, "A merry heart makes a cheerful countenance". [350] "A cheerful heart puts a smile on your face"[351] and "A warm, smiling face reveals a joy-filled heart."[352]

A smile requires no interpreter as it is easily recognised as a global gesture of kindness and acceptance. It enriches those who receive it, without impoverishing those who give it. Studies have shown that a person's smile is their most memorable feature. In fact, while 48 per cent of people will remember your smile, only 25 per cent will remember the first thing you said. [353] Smiling releases endorphins, dopamine and serotonin. Together these neurotransmitters make us feel good from head to toe, prompting a question: Do you smile because you are happy or are you happy because you smile? Smiling activates the release of neuropeptides that work toward fighting off stress. You're actually better-looking when you smile. A study published in the journal

[348] A.A. Milne, treasurequotes.com
[349] Proverbs 15:13 ESV
[350] Proverbs 15:13 NKJV
[351] Proverbs 15:13 TPT
[352] Proverbs 15:13 (VOICE)
[353] Study by the American Academy of Cosmetic Dentistry

Neuropsychologia reported that seeing an attractive, smiling face activates your orbitofrontal cortex, the region in your brain that processes sensory rewards. This suggests that when you view a person smiling, you actually feel rewarded.[354] Babies start smiling in their sleep as soon as they are born. Children smile approximately four hundred times per day, while adults smile an average of twenty times per day. That means between childhood and adulthood we lose three hundred and eighty smiles.

The yellow smiley face icon was designed in 1963 in Massachusetts, when the graphic designer Harvey Ball was commissioned to create a graphic to raise morale among the employees of an insurance company after a series of difficult mergers and acquisitions. Ball finished the design in less than ten minutes and was paid $45 for his work. The image quickly gained popularity, and yellow smiley faces started popping up as a way to convey a beacon of cheer.

Do you have a cheerful expression? Proverbs 15:30 says, "Bright eyes and a cheerful expression bring joy to the heart, and good news revives the spirit and renews health."[355] Do you have a glad heart? "A joyful heart is good medicine".[356]

Salvation through Jesus Christ and our continued relationship with Him is a constant source of joy. The Bible states, "With joy you will draw water from the wells of salvation."[357] Draw from the well. Let Him gladden your heart and make you a beacon of cheer.

---

[354] psychologytoday.com – Facial attractiveness: research Phil Trans R Soc B 12 June, 2011 366: 1638–1659.
[355] Proverbs 15:30 (VOICE)
[356] Proverbs 17:22 ESV
[357] Isaiah 12:2 NIV

52

BIG SHOES TO FILL

"Strength! Courage! Don't be timid; don't get discouraged. God,
your God, is with you every step you take."

Joshua 1:9 MSG

*S*ometimes we refer to "filling someone's shoes", meaning to replace someone in a role, to assume someone's position and responsibilities. If that person excelled at their post, you might say that you "have some big shoes to fill". Joshua had big shoes to fill as God commissioned him in Joshua 1:1–8. We are told, "After the death of Moses the servant of the Lord, it came to pass that the Lord spoke to Joshua the son of Nun, Moses' assistant, saying: "Moses my servant is dead. Now therefore, arise, go over this Jordan, you and all this people, to the land which I am giving to them – the children of Israel."[358] However, God wasn't calling Joshua to be a carbon copy of Moses; Joshua was a unique individual equipped with a skillset from God to carry on His work. God authorised him, "Every place that the sole of your foot will tread upon I have given you".[359] Yes, Joshua had big shoes to fill and a big plan to fulfil but God promised him that He had given Him every place that the sole of "his foot" would tread. This was his calling and the establishing of his goings. This was no vague promise; he even outlined Joshua's area of operation in verse 4.

In like manner God has a unique place and purpose for our lives. The Bible states that, "In his grace, God has given us different gifts for doing certain things well."[360] Don't allow others to impose their personal script on the narrative of your life and reduce you to feeling like an extra

---

[358] Joshua 1:1–2 NKJV
[359] Joshua 1:3 NKJV
[360] Romans 12:6 NLT

in your own story. Let God order your steps, align you with His plans and assign you in your sphere of influence.

God assured Joshua, "I will be with you. I will not leave you nor forsake you."[361] In case Joshua took "cold feet" God emboldened him on four occasions, "Be strong and of good courage;"[362] "Only be strong and very courageous;"[363] "Have I not commanded you? Be strong and of good courage; do not be afraid, nor be dismayed, for the Lord your God is with you wherever you go"[364] and "Only be strong and of good courage."[365]

Courage comes through knowing God and His word. God directed Joshua to be a man of the Word, to observe and do what God had written. "For then you shall make your way prosperous, and then you shall deal wisely and have good success." [366] Revelation of His Word will revolutionise your heart, with repercussions that will reverberate beyond yourself. Take on a stance of courage, tenacity and bravery. As the Bible says, "Be of good courage, and let us behave ourselves valiantly for our people, and for the cities of our God: and let the Lord do that which is good in his sight."[367]

Put your best foot forward; step out with strength and courage. "Strength! Courage! Don't be timid; don't get discouraged. God, your God, is with you every step you take."[368]

[361] Joshua 1:5 NKJV
[362] Joshua 1:6 NKJV
[363] Joshua 1:7 NKJV
[364] Joshua 1:9 NKJV
[365] Joshua 1:18 NKJV
[366] Joshua 1:8 AMPC
[367] 1 Chronicles 19:13 KJV
[368] Joshua 1:9 MSG

53

THE AFFECTIONS OF YOUR HEART

"So above all, guard the affections of your heart, for they affect all that you are. Pay attention to the welfare of your innermost being, for from there flows the wellspring of life."

Proverbs 4:23 TPT

*S*amuel filled his horn with oil and went to the house of Jesse to anoint the next king.[369] As he looked at Jesse's oldest son, Eliab, Samuel was impressed and reckoned this was the man the Lord wanted him to anoint. But God told Samuel, "Do not look at his appearance or at his physical stature, because I have refused him. For the Lord does not see as man sees; for man looks at the outward appearance, but the Lord looks at the heart."[370]

The Lord looks at the heart and that's what I want us to do as well. The Bible tells us, "For the eyes of the Lord move to and fro throughout the earth that He may strongly support those whose heart is completely His."[371] What is God looking for? He is looking for men and women whose hearts are His – completely. To conclude the account of Samuel's mission, Samuel said to Jesse, "Are all the young men here?" Then he said, "There remains yet the youngest, and there he is, keeping the sheep." When he was brought in, the Lord said, "Arise, anoint him; for this is the one!"[372] Why David? Why is he the one? The answer lies in the words, "The Lord has sought for Himself a man after His own heart".[373] A man after His own heart. Those words are key. In the book of Acts, God gave testimony and said, "I have found David the son of

---

[369] 1 Samuel 16
[370] 1 Samuel 16:7 NKJV
[371] 2 Chronicles 16:9 AMP
[372] 1 Samuel 16:11–12 NKJV
[373] 1 Samuel 13:14 NKJV

Jesse, a man after My own heart, who will do all My will."[374] In other translations it reads, "I have found in David, son of Jesse, a man who always pursues my heart and will accomplish all that I have destined him to do."[375] "I have found David son of Jesse a man after My own heart, who will do all My will and carry out My program fully."[376] "I've searched the land and found this David, son of Jesse. He's a man whose heart beats to my heart, a man who will do what I tell him."[377]

Can God say those words of us? I've searched the land and found (put in your name). He is a man whose heart beats to my heart, a man after My own heart, man who will do what I tell him? Or ladies, I've searched the land and found (put in your name). She is a woman whose heart beats to my heart, a woman after My own heart, a woman who will accomplish all that I have destined her to do.

The following verses give us insight into David's heart, "May the words that come out of my mouth and the musings of my heart meet with Your gracious approval"[378] and "Create in me a clean heart, O God, and renew a steadfast spirit within me."[379] Are our hearts clean, pure, unmixed, unalloyed? Free from adhesion to anything that soils and grieves the Spirit of God? "Search me, O God, and know my heart; Try me, and know my anxieties".[380]

---

[374] Acts 13:22NKJV
[375] Acts 13:22 TPT
[376] Acts 13:22 AMPC
[377] Acts 13:22 MSG
[378] Psalm 19:14 VOICE
[379] Psalm 51:10 NKJV
[380] Psalm 139:23 NKJV

54

LUMINARIES OF THE LORD

"Light is sown for the [uncompromisingly] righteous and strewn along their pathway, and joy for the upright in heart [the irrepressible joy which comes from consciousness of His favor and protection]."

Psalm 97:11 AMPC

*H*ave you tried to spot the International Space Station (ISS) as it passes overhead? It is the third brightest object in the sky and easy to spot if you know when to look up. At any given moment, there are up to six humans orbiting 400 km above our heads in this huge science laboratory. Spotting the ISS with the naked eye is a fun and rewarding activity. But have you ever wondered what can be seen from the ISS? Apparently the 2,253-kilometre-long reef off the north-east coast of Australia, the Great Barrier Reef, is visible. Also, hurricanes can be spotted and weather systems tracked. When astronauts glide over London, they can see the iconic river Thames winding through the city of London. The impressive Himalayas, the Grand Canyon in Arizona and the Amazon River are detectable. Also, the world's cities illuminated at night make for some truly beautiful satellite images. The artificial lights are so bright, they seem to create their own constellation.

We are God's children of light on earth. "Rise up in splendor and be radiant, for your light has dawned, and Yahweh's glory now streams from you!"[381] Is His glory streaming from you? Are you radiant? We are here to proclaim the excellencies of Him who called us out of darkness into his marvellous light.[382] We are called to "shine as lights in the world" so that others who now sit in darkness might see the Light of

---

[381] Isaiah 60:1 TPT
[382] 1 Peter 2:9

the World.[383] Jesus said, "You are the light of the world. A city set on a hill cannot be hidden."[384] Your light is not meant to be hidden. Put your light on its stand.

I recall watching a programme about how best to photograph a diamond in order to capture its sparkle and showcase its brilliance. The answer lay in a black background. Against a black backdrop the jewel revealed its radiance. As children of light in a culture of darkness we look to Him and are radiant. We shine with an inner incandescent God-shine. The intensity of our light depends upon the intensity of our walk with Him. John stated, "God is light, and in him is no darkness at all. If we say we have fellowship with him while we walk in darkness, we lie and do not practice the truth. But if we walk in the light, as he is in the light, we have fellowship with one another, and the blood of Jesus his Son cleanses us from all sin."[385] The Bible tells us, "Light is sown for the [uncompromisingly] righteous and strewn along their pathway."[386] The unfolding of His words give us light;[387] the eyes of our hearts are enlightened, that we may know what is the hope to which He has called us.[388] Jesus told us, "I am the light of the world. Whoever follows me will not walk in darkness, but will have the light of life."[389] May we follow the True Light and shine with ever-increasing splendour. You and I will probably never get to be astronauts on the ISS, but together we get to shine as stars in the universe and be the luminaries of the Lord.

---

[383] Philippians 2:15 NKJV
[384] Matthew 5:14 ESV
[385] 1 John 1:5–7 ESV
[386] Psalm 97:11 AMPC
[387] Psalm 119:105
[388] Ephesians 1:18
[389] John 8:12 ESV

55

WHAT ARE YOU MISSING?

"God's invisible qualities – his eternal power and divine nature – have been clearly seen"

Romans 1:20 NIV

oday I want to refer you to the Invisible Gorilla Experiment.[390] Volunteers were asked to watch a video where two groups of people – some dressed in white, others in black – were passing basketballs around. The volunteers were asked to count the passes among players dressed in white while ignoring the passes of those in black. What was astounding was that mid-way through the video about half of watchers totally missed a person in a gorilla suit strolling into the action, facing the camera and pounding its chest before leaving, spending nine seconds on screen. How could something so obvious go completely unnoticed? Most of us would like to think that we're pretty good at paying attention to the world around us – that we're observant, detail-oriented and highly perceptive. But the truth is, we're not. Whether we know it or not, we are all guilty of inattentional blindness.

Think of it this way. God's glory is on display day after day in the skies, with sunrise and sunset showing forth His splendour and countless galaxies and constellations pointing us to the majesty and glory of God. Are we attentive and responsive? The Psalmist says, "The heavens proclaim the glory of God. The skies display his craftsmanship. Day after day they continue to speak; night after night they make him known."[391] The Bible tells us that God's invisible attributes are clearly seen, that "since the creation of the world God's invisible qualities – his eternal power and divine nature – have been clearly seen, being

---

[390] Invisible Gorilla Experiment, Christopher Chabris and Daniel Simons
[391] Psalm 19:1–2 NLT

understood from what has been made, so that people are without excuse".[392] Do we see the panorama of His power?

Let's take another scenario. Are we aware that myriads of mighty angels encircle us and encamp around us? When the king of Syria was aiming to invade and take over Israel, his massive army surrounded the Israelite camp and Elisha's servant was alarmed. He didn't know what to do, so he ran to the prophet Elisha. Elisha said, "Do not fear, for those who are with us are more than those who are with them."[393] Elisha then prayed for God to open his servant's eyes, so he could see the same thing Elisha could see. "Then the Lord opened the eyes of the young man, and he saw. And behold, the mountain was full of horses and chariots of fire all around Elisha."[394] Are we perceptive and discerning of spiritual things? Paul said, "The natural man receiveth not the things of the Spirit of God: for they are foolishness unto him: neither can he know them, because they are spiritually discerned." [395] Are we spiritually discerning?

Are we aware that a great cloud of witnesses in the bandstands of glory are surrounding us and spurring us on? These people have run their race and set us an example of living by faith. We are told, "Therefore, since we are surrounded by such a great cloud of witnesses, let us throw off everything that hinders and the sin that so easily entangles. And let us run with perseverance the race marked out for us, fixing our eyes on Jesus, the pioneer and perfecter of faith." [396] Let us be cognisant, perceptive, wide-awake to what God is doing.

---

[392] Romans 1:20 NIV
[393] 2 Kings 6:16 NKJV
[394] 2 Kings 6:17 NKJV
[395] 1 Corinthians 2:14 KJV
[396] Hebrews 12:1–2 NIV

56

TWO HUNDRED POMEGRANATES!

"The capitals on the two pillars had 200 pomegranates in two rows around them, beside the rounded surface next to the latticework."

1 Kings 7:20 NLT

I must admit that, except for "Read Through the Bible in a Year", I had not lingered for long in 1 Kings 7, a chapter which intricately details the Temple furnishings and reveals an obscure artisan called Huram, who was responsible for the finishing touches to the Temple. We are told, "King Solomon then asked for a man named Huram to come from Tyre … Huram was extremely skillful and talented in any work in bronze, and he came to do all the metal work for King Solomon."[397]

The exact work is detailed in the rest of the chapter. We are told how he cast two twenty-seven-feet-tall pillars to adorn the entrance and named them "Jachin" (meaning, "He shall establish") and "Boaz" (meaning, "In Him is strength").[398] These pillars would attract attention upon arrival and remind the worshippers as they entered God's House that this was where His people were established in the faith and in relationship with Him and that they derived their strength from the Lord. Huram also designed seven-and-a-half-feet capitals to place on top of the pillars. These were embellished with lily-work. Then on top of the capitals there were two hundred pomegranates in two rows around them.[399] Can you imagine the painstaking effort required to handcraft two hundred pomegranates on top of these columns? Why did he even bother? After all, they were positioned over thirty-four feet high and

---

[397] 1 King 7:13–14 NLT
[398] 1 Kings 7::15 & 2 Chronicles 3:17
[399] 1 Kings 7:20

highly unlikely to be seen from the ground. He could have left that part plain since no one would notice, not even Solomon. They would really only be visible to God and the artisan himself. Therein lies the point. He did his most intricate work with excellence for God. His work was not just artwork but worship. He honed his skills for the honour of God. It is very easy to live as one who gives "eye-service" for the attention of other people. But what about God's eyes?

God has anointed and gifted each one of us with a skillset that can make this world a more beautiful place. "God has given each of us the ability to do certain things well."[400] He is your audience. His approval is what counts. After all, what matters most and in fact the only thing that matters, is to hear His words, " Well done my good and faithful servant."[401] Paul shares a simple but liberating message in the following verses, which help us to develop an "audience of one" mindset: "Work with enthusiasm, as though you were working for the Lord rather than for people;"[402] "whatever you do, do it all for the glory of God"[403] and "Whatever you do, work heartily, as for the Lord and not for men, knowing that from the Lord you will receive the inheritance as your reward. You are serving the Lord Christ."[404]

Life becomes remarkably easier when we do everything as to the Lord, and our love for Him is the driving force. I remember hearing someone say the wise words, "How you do anything is how you do everything." Isn't that so true? It even applies to doing dishes! Whatever you do … do it for God.

---

[400] Romans 12:6 LB
[401] Matthew 25:21 NLT
[402] Ephesians 6:7 NLT
[403] 1 Corinthians 10:31 NLT
[404] Colossians 3:23–24 ESV

57

PRAY MUCH, ACCOMPLISH MUCH

"The effective, fervent prayer of a righteous man avails much."
James 5:16 NKJV

For many believers, prayer is simply an afterthought. If we've tried everything else, we might as well pray, it can't hurt. For James, prayer was his first response and it is said that he acquired the nickname of "Camel knees" because of the callouses on his knees from hours devoted to daily prayer. James gave us the verse, "The effective, fervent prayer of a righteous man avails much."[405]

I have referenced this particular verse in many different settings. Sometimes I have put emphasis on the word "effective", showing that in Greek it is "energoumene", conveying the idea of "energetic" dynamic prayer. Effective prayer relies on the Spirit's leading and empowerment. I have also accentuated the word "fervent" and shown how prayer ought to be ardent, earnest and intense, as in the exemplar of the early church. On occasion I have highlighted the word "prayer", in Greek "deisis", and encouraged God's people to strongly beseech Him to move and to meet their specific need. "Deisis" reveals a humble attitude and a deep dependency on God. I have also spotlighted the word "righteous" in the verse and assured believers that because they are "made righteous" in Christ, their prayers are heard and tremendous power is made available. When it comes to prayer, too many feel under-qualified and overwhelmed, not realising that the price has been paid and access given for each one of us to approach the throne of grace with boldness.

---

[405] James 5:16 NKJV

Moving along our verse, I have touched from time to time on the word "avail", the original word meaning "to be a force" and "prevail". The only word I have left unmentioned is the last one, "much". It is the Greek word "polus" meaning as translated "much", "great in amount or extent, multitudinous". Do you believe that your prayers avail *much*? They are not just making a little bit of a difference, they avail MUCH! They are affecting outcomes. If only God's people had the deeper revelation of this, then prayer would become fundamental, not supplemental in our lives. As the New Living Translation says, "The earnest prayer of a righteous person has great power and produces wonderful results."[406] It is as simple as: pray much, accomplish much. When a believing person prays, great things happen.[407] The energetic prayers of a person made right with God are a potent force in petitioning the Almighty power of God to accomplish His Kingdom's purposes on earth. Prayer is powerful because God is powerful; and prayer is the means through which the divine power is released and channelled into our lives. I leave you with a couple of quotes from saints of the past to ponder:

"Prayer is the key that unlocks all the storehouses of God's infinite grace and power. All that God is and all that God has is at the disposal of prayer, but we must use the key."[408]

"The power of prayer can never be overrated. They who cannot serve God by preaching need not regret. If a man can but pray he can do anything. He who knows how to overcome with God in prayer has Heaven and earth at his disposal."[409]

God acts powerfully and effectively through the prayers of His people. What an amazing arrangement – God partnering with human beings to accomplish His purposes.

---

[406] James 5:16 NLT
[407] James 5:16 NCV
[408] *The Power of Prayer and the Prayer of Power*, R.A. Torrey (Revell, 1924, p. 25.)
[409] C.H. Spurgeon (quotessayings.net)

58

ABUNDANT FRESH FRUIT

"But the fruit of the Spirit is love, joy, peace, patience, kindness, goodness, faithfulness, gentleness, self-control"

Galatians 5:22–23 ESV

I love fresh fruit, my favourite being a delicious, sweet nectarine. Lately I have been finding out that there is a lot more to fruit than I thought. For example, did you know that the study of fruit is called pomology? I found out that a banana is not a fruit, it is a herb, and apples, peaches and raspberries are all members of the rose family! I learned that drinking grapefruit juice while taking some prescription medications can cause instant overdose and even death. Also, that square watermelons are grown by Japanese farmers for easier stack and store. Then, and I had to double-check this one to verify its truth, there is a tree called the fruit salad tree which grows up to six different fruits on the same tree. What's more, all the fruits on it retain their own characteristic flavour, appearance and ripening times!

The Bible speaks a lot about fruit. To give you a flavour: John the Baptist said, "Produce fruit in keeping with repentance."[410] Jesus stated, "The tree is known by its fruit." [411] Again, "When your lives bear abundant fruit, you demonstrate that you are my mature disciples who glorify my Father!"[412] and "You did not choose Me but I chose you, and appointed you that you would go and bear fruit, and that your fruit would remain."[413]

---

[410] Matthew 3:8 NIV
[411] Matthew 12:33 NKJV
[412] John 15:8 TPT
[413] John 15:16 NKJV

Paul prayed for us to be "filled with the fruit of righteousness that comes through Jesus Christ, to the glory and praise of God".[414]

When I heard of the fruit salad tree with its display of various fruits, the Scripture which came to mind was Galatians 5:22–23, "But the fruit of the Spirit is love, joy, peace, patience, kindness, goodness, faithfulness, gentleness, self-control."[415] The Spirit produces in us the fruit or evidence of His work. The Amplified Bible phrases it, "But the fruit of the [Holy] Spirit [the work which His presence within accomplishes] is love, joy (gladness), peace, patience (an even temper, forbearance), kindness, goodness (benevolence), faithfulness, gentleness (meekness, humility), self-control (self-restraint, continence)."[416]

It is easy to love sometimes. It is easy to be joyful sometimes. It is easy to be patient, sometimes. But what about an ongoing consistency in every season? Check out how the Message Bible speaks of the fruit appearing in our orchard, "affection for others, exuberance about life, serenity. We develop a willingness to stick with things, a sense of compassion in the heart, and a conviction that a basic holiness permeates things and people. We find ourselves involved in loyal commitments, not needing to force our way in life, able to marshal and direct our energies wisely". [417] Genuine fruit is produced from within and Galatians 5 shows us how to live by the Spirit, be led by the Spirit, and keep in step with the Spirit. [418]

---

[414] Philippians 1:11 ESV
[415] Galatians 5:22–23 ESV
[416] Galatians 5:22–23 AMPC
[417] Galatians 5:22–23 MSG
[418] Galatians 5:16.18, 25

59

IN A SPIN

"For you are the children of your father the devil and you love to do the evil things he does. He was a murderer from the beginning and a hater of truth – there is not an iota of truth in him. When he lies, it is perfectly normal; for he is the father of liars."

John 8:44 LB

I was thinking of the word "spin" lately. Spin is a form of propaganda, achieved through knowingly providing a biased interpretation of an event. A spin doctor is one who manipulates information and deliberately deceives. Someone can put their "spin" on a story. Things can "spin" out of control. We might talk about being "in a spin" when we are worried about something. The origin of the word "spin" comes from Old English "spinnan" meaning to draw and twist fibres into yarn. Politicians are adept at "spinning" the details of a story to advance their own agenda. The devil is too. He spins his own agenda as a master of deception and the father of lies. "When he speaks a lie, he speaks from his own resources, for he is a liar and the father of it."[419]

It's often said that the mind is the devil's playground. No wonder the Bible says, "Be careful how you think; your life is shaped by your thoughts."[420] All it takes is a thought injected into your mind in the middle of the night and soon the mind can go into overdrive as he spins his yarn, twisting his lies into the narrative of our lives and leaving us in a spin of spiralling emotions. He often presents a bit of reality – perhaps a real struggle, symptom or circumstance – and then fills in the unknowns with imaginations. Those imaginations are the fodder for your fears, insecurities and sense of condemnation. Paul speaks of,

---

[419] John 8:44 NKJV
[420] Proverbs 4:23 GNT

"Casting down imaginations, and every high thing that exalteth itself against the knowledge of God, and bringing into captivity every thought to the obedience of Christ."[421]

When speaking of anxiety, a state of being in a spin, Jesus said, "Take no thought".[422] Then He directed us to observe the birds and lilies, "Consider the lilies of the field, how they grow; they toil not, neither do they spin".[423] Are you in a spin over something? The Bible tells us what to do, "Do not be anxious about anything, but in every situation, by prayer and petition, with thanksgiving, present your requests to God. And the peace of God, which transcends all understanding, will guard your hearts and your minds in Christ Jesus."[424] Then Paul adds, "Whatever is true ... noble ... right ... pure ... lovely ... admirable ... excellent ... praiseworthy – think about such things."[425]

We can select our thoughts. As Max Lucado put it, "You are the air traffic controller of your mental airport. You occupy the control tower, directing the mental traffic of your world. If a thought lands, it is because you gave it permission. If it leaves, it is because you commanded it to do so. You select your thoughts."[426]

Deliberately deliberate on what liberates us! Jesus said, "And you shall know the truth, and the truth shall make you free."[427] Put on the belt of Truth, steady yourself in His Word, stay your mind on Him and experience His perfect peace.

---

[421] 2 Corinthians 10:5 KJV

[422] Matthew 6:25 KJV

[423] Matthew 6 :28 KJV

[424] Philippians 4:6–7 NIV

[425] Philippians 4:8

[426] Max Lucado, June, 2016 sermon: "Your problem isn't your problem."

[427] John 8:32 NKJV

60

THE REGENT HONEYEATER

"One generation commends your works to another; they tell of your mighty acts"

Psalm 145:4: NIV

I'm not sure what exactly drew my attention to it – whether it was its name, "The Regent Honeyeater", or the striking picture of a distinctive yellow and black plumaged bird. Either way the headline stood out as I browsed through the newsfeed on my phone. It stated, "Regent honeyeater: Endangered bird has forgotten its song."[428]

The regent honeyeater is a rare songbird native to south-eastern Australia. Once seen in flocks of hundreds, it is now critically endangered and there are thought to be only three hundred individual songbirds left in the wild. Because their population has crashed to such low numbers and they are sparsely spread over large terrain, young males are unable to locate adult males and are not getting a chance to learn calls and songs from them. These nectar-feeding songbirds learn in a similar way to how we acquire our linguistic ability and fluency through association. Dr Ross Crates, an ecologist, has been studying them. During his research he noticed that instead of their soft, warbling song produced with characteristic head-bobbing, they were singing what he called "weird songs". They were picking up the calls of other bird species such as noisy friarbirds, currawongs and cuckoo-shrikes and imitating them.

When I read this, I thought of the importance of association as believers, the "one another" Scriptures which are so prevalent in the New Testament, and our responsibility to communicate the Gospel

---

[428] https://www.bbc.co.uk/news/science-environment-56417544 17 March 2021

message to the next generation. Otherwise, they will pick what the repertoire of what the world around them is saying and utter the dialect of doom rather than the language of life. The Bible states, "One generation commends your works to another; they tell of your mighty acts".[429]

In the book of Judges we read of what happens when we fail to communicate our faith. "So the people served the Lord all the days of Joshua, and all the days of the elders who outlived Joshua, who had seen all the great works of the Lord which He had done for Israel. Now Joshua the son of Nun, the servant of the Lord, died when he was one hundred and ten years old … When all that generation had been gathered to their fathers, another generation arose after them who did not know the Lord nor the work which He had done for Israel."[430]

Are you leaving a legacy of faith and discipling others? Are you telling them of the goodness and grace of God, so that they can sing salvation's song? The Psalmist declared, "Even when I am old and gray, do not forsake me, my God, till I declare your power to the next generation, your mighty acts to all who are to come."[431] A psalm of Asaph reads, "So the next generation might know them – even the children not yet born – and they in turn will teach their own children. So each generation should set its hope anew on God, not forgetting his glorious miracles and obeying his commands."[432]

The onus is on us, as Peter puts it, "But you are the ones chosen by God, chosen for the high calling of priestly work, chosen to be a holy people, God's instruments to do his work and speak out for him, to tell others of the night-and-day difference he made for you – from nothing to something, from rejected to accepted."[433]

---

[429] Psalm 145:4 NIV
[430] Judges 2:7–8,10 NKJV
[431] Psalm 71:18 NIV
[432] Psalm 78:6–7 NLT
[433] 1 Peter 2:9 MSG

61

IMAGINE DEL CUORE

"Return to the stronghold, you prisoners of hope. Even today I declare that I will restore double to you."

Zechariah 9:12 NKJV

*I*t was an abandoned block of marble. An unfinished project. Neglected for over twenty-five years. Previously worked on by two other artists, Agostino di Duccio (in 1464) and Antonio Rossellino (in 1475), both artists had abandoned their work after noticing imperfections in the marble's grain. Yet despite these flaws, Michelangelo took up the monumental challenge of carving the biblical hero David. Almost four years of his life were consumed with breathing his artistry into the block. As he chiselled, he envisioned what he called "imagine del cuore" or image of the heart. His task was to remove the excess stone so that the statue of "David" could be liberated. He didn't focus on the flaws, he foresaw the final outcome, a masterpiece. The statue can be viewed at the Galleria dell'Accademia in Florence. Tourists flock to see it but often overlook the other unfinished (non finiti) statues in the Hall. These Michelangelo called prisoners or captives.

The Bible tells us of the manifesto of the Messiah, "He has sent Me to announce release to the captives".[434] Speaking through the prophet Zechariah, God refers to His hearers as "prisoners of hope" saying "Return to the stronghold, you prisoners of hope. Even today I declare that I will restore double to you."[435]

Do you remember what Jeremiah had recorded some years previously? "For I know the plans I have for you," declares the Lord, "plans to prosper you and not to harm you, plans to give you hope and

---

[434] Luke 4:18 AMPC
[435] Zechariah 9:12 NKJV

a future."[436] Thank God that, "In his great mercy he has given us new birth into a living hope through the resurrection of Jesus Christ from the dead."[437]

He is gentle to remove the excess stone we carry, to chisel us into the person He desires to see and to reveal more and more of His Son in us day by day. As Michelangelo chipped away whatever did not look like David, so may the Master Artist shear off all that is superfluous and surplus to His purpose in us. We are His masterpiece. As Paul said, "For we are God's masterpiece. He has created us anew in Christ Jesus, so we can do the good things he planned for us long ago."[438] Long before we were conceived by our parents, we took shape in the imagination of the Almighty. As he said to Jeremiah, "Before I shaped you in the womb, I knew all about you. Before you saw the light of day, I had holy plans for you: A prophet to the nations – that's what I had in mind for you."[439] He has holy plans for us as well. God is "working in us that which is pleasing in his sight".[440] What's more, "And I am certain that God, who began the good work within you, will continue his work until it is finally finished on the day when Christ Jesus returns."[441]

Perhaps you feel like an abandoned block of marble or an unfinished project, others having tried to carve you into their imagination. Perhaps others have pointed out your imperfections and looked on you as a lost cause. If so, allow God to reveal His heart for you. Let Him breathe His grace, strength, hope, and peace into you. Engage with His Word and encounter His heart for you. That way, you'll not only discover God's heart for you but also discover and develop your own heart of love for Him.

---

[436] Jeremiah 29: 11 NIV
[437] 1 Peter 1:3 NIV
[438] Ephesians 2:10 NLT
[439] Jeremiah 1:5 MSG
[440] Hebrews 13:21 ESV
[441] Philippians 1:6 NLT

62

DAY BY DAY

"You saw me before I was born. Every day of my life was recorded in your book. Every moment was laid out before a single day had passed. How precious are your thoughts about me, O God. They cannot be numbered! I can't even count them; they outnumber the grains of sand! And when I wake up, you are still with me!"

Psalm 139:16–18 NLT

*D*id you know there's a word for hitting the snooze button over and over? It's called "drockling". It's a technical term for not only hitting the snooze button but also drifting in and out of sleep in the early morning. A few extra minutes of sleep can be appealing, but drockling confuses your body's internal clock making it hard to wake up refreshed. Experts say that when you finally do roll out of bed, you're more likely to have that groggy feeling called sleep inertia.

How do you rise and shine? Listen to what the Psalmist says in our verses today. When he wakes up, he awakens to the purpose of God and the Presence of God. He says, "Every day of my life was recorded in your book. Every moment was laid out before a single day had passed" and "When I wake up, you are still with me!"[442]

The child of God never awakens to a day unscripted or unaccompanied. I encourage you to awaken to Divine purpose every morning and begin to live each day with a sense of excitement and fulfilment. Realise the significance of each day and make it count. The Bible tells us, "Surely goodness and mercy shall follow me all the days of my life".[443] That includes today. Welcome His goodness and mercy every day. Treasure each day as a gift from God. From time to time, I

---

[442] Psalm 139:16,18 NLT
[443] Psalm 23:6 NKJV

have taken a bar of delicious dark chocolate into my study and eaten it without realising. Having become so absorbed in whatever task I was finishing, I missed out on luxuriating in the richness of the cocoa and that smooth melt in the mouth experience. All I had was evidence of an empty wrapper. The same can happen to our days. Ever wonder where our days go?

In the Living Bible Psalm 139:16 states, "You saw me before I was born and scheduled each day of my life before I began to breathe. Every day was recorded in your book!"[444] This very day for you is scheduled in God's almanac. It would be felony to fritter it away by fretting over yesterday's failures or fussing over tomorrow's assignments. Today matters to God. Ask yourself, When are God's mercies made new? *Every morning.*[445] When should you rejoice and be glad? *Today. This is the day.*[446] How often do you depend on Him for sustenance and bread? *This day. Daily bread.*[447] How often do you take up your cross? *Daily.*[448] How often are you inwardly renewed? *Day by day.*[449] I recall back in school singing and swaying to the rhythm of "Day by day" from the musical *Godspell.* I later found out that the words were based on a prayer by Richard of Chichester, "May I know Thee more clearly, love Thee more dearly, and follow Thee more nearly, day by day. Amen."[450] Isn't that a beautiful prayer? Awaken to His Presence and appreciate each day as an opportunity to journey life with Him.

---

[444] Psalm 139:16 LB
[445] Lamentations 3:22
[446] Psalm 118:24
[447] Matthew 6:11
[448] Luke 9:23
[449] 2 Corinthians 4:16
[450] Richard, Bishop of Chichester (1197–1253)

63

ANYTHING AGAINST ANYONE

"And when you assume the posture of prayer, remember that it's not all asking. If you have anything against someone, forgive"

Mark 11:25 MSG

Mark tells us about the time when Jesus was conversing with the disciples and stated, "Therefore I tell you, whatever you ask in prayer, believe that you have received it, and it will be yours."[451] Then Jesus said, "And whenever you stand praying, forgive, if you have anything against anyone".[452] Another version reads, "And when you assume the posture of prayer, remember that it's not all asking. If you have anything against someone, forgive".[453] Ponder those words, "Anything against anyone".

If you were to look in my Bible you would see that I have underlined, highlighted, asterisked and even placed a shiny star sticker beside verse 24! You can tell that I love this verse. It speaks of asking, believing and receiving. Yet the following verse is strangely unmarked. No underlining. No highlighting. No lustrous luminary next to it. God however has underscored it in my heart. I love how the Passion Translation gives expression to it, "And whenever you stand praying, if you find that you carry something in your heart against another person, release him and forgive him so that your Father in heaven will also release you and forgive you of your faults."

God is lavish with His forgiveness! Aren't we glad? However, just as God is lavish with forgiveness, He is also uncompromising about our forgiving others. Before you pray, search your heart and see if there is anything holed up there that doesn't belong. Invite God to reveal to you

---

[451] Mark 11:24 ESV
[452] Mark 11:25 ESV
[453] Mark 11:25 MSG

things you've brushed aside but never dealt with. Choose to let the little things go so that no root of bitterness or unforgiveness springs up. C.S. Lewis stated, "Everyone says forgiveness is a lovely idea, until they have something to forgive."[454] What should we do if we have anything against anyone? "Forgive him and let it drop (leave it, let it go)."[455] Paul phrased it, "Make allowance for each other's faults, and forgive anyone who offends you. Remember, the Lord forgave you, so you must forgive others."[456] Also, "Lay aside bitter words, temper tantrums, revenge, profanity, and insults. But instead be kind and affectionate toward one another. Has God graciously forgiven you? Then graciously forgive one another in the depths of Christ's love."[457]

Jesus gives us a beautiful definition of forgiveness, "And even if he sins against you seven times in a day, and turns to you seven times and says, I repent [I am sorry], you must forgive him (give up resentment and consider the offence as recalled and annulled)."[458] Give up resentment and consider the offence as recalled and annulled.

Lest we still somehow stintingly withhold forgiveness or miss the point, Jesus tells the story of a king who forgave one of his servants a huge financial obligation, only to learn that the same servant had subsequently forced a fellow attendant into prison for not repaying him a minuscule amount. Infuriated, the king turned the unforgiving servant over to the torturers. Jesus concludes by saying, "So also my heavenly Father will do to every one of you, if you do not forgive your brother from your heart."[459] Let us remember, when we assume the posture of prayer, that it's not all asking. If you have anything against someone, forgive.

---

454 C.S. Lewis, *Mere Christianity* (1943)
455 Mark 11:25 AMPC
456 Colossians 3:13 NLT
457 Ephesians 4: 31–32 TPT
458 Luke 17:4 AMPC
459 Matthew 18:35 ESV

64

TURNING THE WORLD UPSIDE DOWN

"'Paul and Silas have caused trouble all over the world,' they shouted, 'and now they are here disturbing our city, too.'"

Acts 17:6 NLT

*W*hat is the ideal room temperature? It is common for members of the same household to prefer different temperatures – I know! Some people love the comfort of living in sweltering Sahara-like heat and others prefer glacial Arctic tundra-like conditions, with most of us sitting somewhere in the middle. This makes the question of, "What is the ideal room temperature?" a difficult one to answer. Apparently, the best ambient temperature for your home is usually between 18–20°C all year round. Whatever the season, it is recommended that you use a thermostat to monitor it.

In 1963, Dr. Martin Luther King Jr. wrote his "Letter from Birmingham Jail". Addressing an acculturated church, acclimatised to the world, adrift in a sea of mediocrity, he wrote the stirring words, "There was a time when the church was very powerful – in the time when the early Christians rejoiced at being deemed worthy to suffer for what they believed. In those days the church was not merely a thermometer that recorded the ideas and principles of popular opinion; it was a thermostat that transformed the mores of society."[460]

A thermometer is a passive agent that merely reflects the climate around it. A thermostat is an active agent that works toward changing and regulating the climate. The challenge is this – are we in thermometer mode, going with the flow of popular opinion, conforming and fitting in, merely projecting the temperature that society has already set? Or are we operating in thermostat mode, intentionally changing the temperature? Where in your life are you telling the temperature? What

---

[460] Dr. Martin Luther King Jr, "Letter from Birmingham Jail", an open letter written on 16 April, 1963.

parts are simply mirroring culture? What parts of your life are you altering the atmosphere as a thermostat? When you walk into a room, do you adapt to or alter the atmosphere with love, joy, peace, kindness and gentleness?

King's letter continues, "Wherever the early Christians entered a town the power structure got disturbed and immediately sought to convict them for being 'disturbers of the peace' and 'outside agitators'. But they went on with the conviction that they were 'a colony of heaven' and had to obey God rather than man. They were small in number but big in commitment." King wrote, "So often the contemporary church is a weak, ineffectual voice with an uncertain sound. So often it is an arch supporter of the status quo. Far from being disturbed by the presence of the church, the power structure of the average community is consoled by the church's silent and often even vocal sanction of things as they are." His parting warning is this, "If the church of today does not recapture the sacrificial spirit of the early church, it will lose its authentic ring, forfeit the loyalty of millions, and be dismissed as an irrelevant social club with no meaning for the twentieth century."

What a wake-up call! What a reality check! Rise up believers, emboldened by Jesus. When Paul and his companions entered Thessalonica, they made an impact. One translation reads, "They've shown up on our doorstep, attacking everything we hold dear!"[461] They disturbed the status quo. "Those troublemakers who have turned the world upside down have come here to our city."[462] Let's affect the culture with Christ. Let's become missional, visional, functional and expressional again.

---

[461] Acts 17:6 MSG
[462] Acts 17:6 TPT

65

OUT OF ORDER

"Order my steps in thy word."

Psalm 11:133 KJV

"Out of order". When we hear these words they can refer to various situations. They can signify that something is not working properly. I recall one memorable holiday abroad where our room was on the sixth floor and the sign on the lift read, "Out of order". It was out of commission, not in service, inoperable and we would have to hoof it up the stairs. "Out of order" can also refer to inappropriate behaviour. If it is said, "He/she was well out of order", it is implied that what was said or done was unacceptable or unfair. Out of order can also mean that something is not in sequence. For example, if I want to withdraw money from the ATM, I not only need to know the correct four-digit pin, but also know the numbers in the right order. If I want to telephone someone, it matters that the numbers I dial are again in sequence.

Today's verse tells us, "Order my steps in thy word." Or, "Direct my footsteps according to your word." [463] This lengthy psalm of one hundred and seventy-six verses has a cohesive narrative which references and celebrates the powerful effect of the Word of God, bringing order to our lives. The Hebrew word for "order" can be translated as direct, set straight, or firmly establish. The Psalmist is recognising that there is indeed a right way, a correct ordering in the way we should go. A few verses earlier it was stated, "Your word is a lamp for my steps; it lights the path before me."[464] God knows what we

---

[463] Psalm 119:133 NIV
[464] Psalm 119:105 VOICE

need to stay on course. Another translation reads, "Your words are a flashlight to light the path ahead of me and keep me from stumbling."[465]

Don't overlook God's confirmations and His flashes of light to bring vision to your path. As you open His word and read it with an open heart, He breaks open His Word and gives you the light needed to navigate the necessary steps ahead. As Psalm 119:130 states, "Break open your Word within me until revelation-light shines out! Those with open hearts are given insight into your plans."[466] He continues, "I open my mouth and inhale the Word of God because I crave the revelation of your commands."[467]

Is this describing your attitude to God's Word? We do not want our lives to be out of order, out of commission, out of service; or behave in a way deemed unworthy or unfair in the sight of God. Nor do we want to fail to make withdrawals from our Heavenly Father, our Source and Sustainer. Let Him order your steps and instruct you in the way you should go. Here's a great template prayer, "Cause me to hear Your loving-kindness in the morning, for on You do I lean and in You do I trust. Cause me to know the way wherein I should walk, for I lift up my inner self to You."[468] Here's another, "I'm your servant – help me understand what that means, the inner meaning of your instructions."[469]

Let's not miss the comfort, hope, perspective, wisdom and direction He has for us. Let's ingest His insight for living. I encourage you to journal the journey each day so that you can look back and celebrate the faithfulness of God and the ordering of your steps.

---

[465] Psalm 119:105 TLB
[466] Psalm 119:130 TPT
[467] Psalm 119:131 TPT
[468] Psalm 143:8 AMPC
[469] Psalm 119:125 MSG

66

SAUSAGE DELIGHT

"Then I will go to the altar of God, to God, my joy and my delight."
Psalm 43:4 NIV

I remember when we were newly married and on a limited budget, I concocted a meal (randomly threw in a selection of tasty ingredients and blended a sauce) and I called it Sausage Delight! After all, there's Angel Delight and Turkish Delight and Sunny Delight. Why not Sausage Delight? Well, Alistair loved the dish and requested it again and again. It was only when we went to a restaurant some months later and he asked the waiter if they had Sausage Delight that I had to admit that the "culinary delicacy" wasn't known beyond the confines of our home!

Let me ask you, what would you reference with the word "delight"? The Psalmist used it when speaking of how much God's Word meant to him. "I delight in your decrees; I will not neglect your word."[470] Again, "Your statutes are my delight; they are my counselors."[471] God's Word brought him great delight as we see throughout the psalms. He said, "I rejoice at thy word, as one that findeth great spoil".[472] This speaks of such discovery and rich reward.

Do you see God's Word as treasure just waiting to be unearthed and explored and enjoyed on a daily basis? Do you bounce out of bed with the expectation of encountering God in the sacred pages? Psalm 19:10 tells us, "The rarest treasures of life are found in his truth. That's why God's Word is prized like others prize the finest gold. Sweeter also than honey are his living words – sweet words dripping from the

---

[470] Psalm 119:16 NIV
[471] Psalm 119:24 NIV
[472] Psalm 119:162 KJV

honeycomb."[473] Sweeter than honey, better than gold. Check out this effervescent exclamation of delight in God's words, "The law of Your mouth is better to me than thousands of coins of gold and silver."[474] Or, "The words you speak to me are worth more than all the riches and wealth in the whole world!"[475]

Passionately he declared, "I pant with expectation, longing for your commands." [476] The Message Bible phrases it, "Mouth open and panting, I wanted your commands more than anything."[477] More than anything? We are beginning to see how much God's words delighted him. This verse says it all, "I treasure your every word to me."[478] Can we say the same?

The Psalmist also delighted in God's presence. He affirmed, "Then I will go to the altar of God, to God, my joy and my delight."[479] The original Hebrew of this verse employs an idiom that might be translated literally, I will go to "the God of the joy of my joy". There is a doubling up of the joy, using two Hebrew words that are similar in meaning, emphasising the joy felt by the Psalmist as he comes into God's presence. The joy and delight he experiences before God is impressive, profuse and intense. No wonder we are told, "Better is one day in your courts than a thousand elsewhere".[480] You can sense what a single day in the presence of God meant to the writer. Another translation puts it, "One day spent in your house, this beautiful place of worship, beats thousands spent on Greek island beaches."[481] Delighting in Him far exceeds anything this world has to offer. I encourage you, "Take delight in the Lord."[482]

---

[473] Psalm 19:10 TPT
[474] Psalm 119:72 NKJV
[475] Psalm 119:72 TPT
[476] Psalm 119:131 NLT
[477] Psalm 119:131 MSG
[478] Psalm 119:55 TPT
[479] Psalm 43:4 NIV
[480] Psalm 84:10 NIV
[481] Psalm 84:10 MSG
[482] Psalm 37:4 NIV

67

THROUGH THE WINDOW

"Search me, O God, and know my heart; try me, and know my anxieties; and see if there is any wicked way in me, and lead me in the way everlasting."

Psalm 139:23–24 NLT

*I*n my pre-school years I watched a programme called *Playschool*. It fascinated me because there was a square, a round and an arched window; the young viewers were invited to guess which window would be chosen that day. Years later I came across the Johari Window, a model of interpersonal awareness sometimes used in the corporate environment to improve individual and team performance. It consists of four quadrants or panes. The first quadrant is the Arena Quadrant. It's your public persona, your Facebook feed, the information about you known to you and those around you. The second quadrant is referred to as the Blindspot. It consists of those things others know about you, but you don't know about you. The information can be positive or negative and include hidden strengths or areas for improvement. The third quadrant is referred to as the Facade, where information is known to the individual, but not known to anyone else. This is who you are when no one is looking. This may consist of private information, which the individual chooses to keep hidden. The last pane is the Unknown quadrant and it consists of those things you don't know about you and others don't know about you.

God knows you better than you know you. In Psalm 139 this is abundantly clear from the very first words David penned, "O Lord, You have searched me and known me".[483] He declared, "You are acquainted with all my ways."[484] He affirmed, "You saw who you created me to be

---

[483] Psalm 139:1 NKJV
[484] Psalm 139:3 AMPC

before I became me!"[485] It's in a final verse that David prays, "Search me, O God, and know my heart; try me, and know my anxieties; and see if there is any wicked way in me, and lead me in the way everlasting."[486] This provides a powerful prayer for anyone brave enough to pray it.

– *Know my heart.* God not only knows your public persona and your blind spots. He can see through the facade and even know what's unknown about you. God probes beyond the epidermis to disclose the intentions of the heart. He presses past the camouflage to confront your unresolved issues and bring healing. When David says, "Search me O God", the word for "search" is "chaqar". This has the meaning "to probe, to do a thorough search". David wants to see himself as God sees him so that he knows what he needs to change in his life. What will God see if He searches your heart? Are there things you have been trying to hide that need to be rooted out and dealt with?

– *Know my anxieties.* What will God find as He tries your thoughts? Are there strongholds of doubts, insecurities, stress and anxieties that need to be purged from your mind?

– *See if there is any wicked way in me.* Or "offensive way" (NIV). Or "grievous way" (ESV). The word David chose, "otseb", can mean pain, sorrow or even an idol. The focus appears to be on the grief David would cause to God by his wrong behaviour. Are you willing to change the things in our lives that are grievous to Him?

– *Lead me in the way everlasting.* Follow His leading. Walk with Him and allow Him to direct your path. Surrender to Him, believing His infinite understanding of who you are is far more superior than your finite perspective.

---

[485] Psalm 139:16 TPT
[486] Psalm 139:23–24 NLT

68

DON'T MERIMNATE!

"Don't worry about anything; instead, pray about everything."
Philippians 4:6 NLT

Interestingly, I discovered that the Bible is Kindle's most highlighted book, and Philippians 4:6–7 is the most highlighted passage. Let's check out verse 6 today. "Do not be anxious about anything, but in every situation, by prayer and petition, with thanksgiving, present your requests to God."[487]

This is clear cut – do not be anxious about anything. Be anxious for nothing. Entertain no anxious cares. "Merimnate" is the Greek word for "anxious" – M-E-R-I-M-N-A-T-E. It sounds like the English word "marinate". If you marinate in the wrong thoughts, you're eventually going to be full of all kinds of fear and apprehension. The Bible tells us again and again not to worry. Proverbs 12:25 states, "Anxiety in a man's heart weighs him down."[488] Odds are, wherever you are today, there is something worrying you in your life right now, whether it is personal, family-related or on a national level. Anxiety can be like a meteor shower of what ifs of worry, leaving us with an apprehensive trail of disquiet and fragmented fireworks of fear and astronomical angst. How can we prevail over worry? Here's the answer, "Don't worry about anything; instead, pray about everything."[489]

Rather than rehearse the churning chaos threatening to congest your cerebral cortex, refresh yourself in the sovereignty of God, anchoring yourself in His character. Pause to ask yourself, what part of God's character do you need to trust more? Assured of His sovereignty, then approach the throne of God's grace with confidence. What prayer do

---

[487] Philippians 4:6 NIV
[488] Proverbs 12:25 ESV
[489] Philippians 4:6 NLT

138

you need to put between your worry and your peace? "Don't fret or worry. Instead of worrying, pray. Let petitions and praises shape your worries into prayers, letting God know your concerns. Before you know it, a sense of God's wholeness, everything coming together for good, will come and settle you down. It's wonderful what happens when Christ displaces worry at the center of your life."[490] Try it for yourself. Shape your worries into prayers. Let Christ displace the worry at the centre of your life. If worry is at the centre, Christ is marginalised. If Christ is at the centre, worry is replaced by peace and anxious thoughts by a sense of God's wholeness. I don't know what you're worried about, but the answer is the same in every situation. The answer is Jesus. Peter told us, "Cast all your anxiety on him because he cares for you."[491] Or as J.B. Phillips' translation reads, "You can throw the whole weight of your anxieties upon him, for you are his personal concern."

Isn't that lovely – *you* are His personal concern. Offload your cargo of concern and allow Him to give you peace and perspective. "His peace will keep your thoughts and your hearts quiet and at rest as you trust in Christ Jesus."[492]

---

[490] Philippians 4:6–7 MSG
[491] 1 Peter 5:7 NIV
[492] Philippians 4:7 LB

69.

IDIOMS FROM AROUND THE WORLD

"Woe to you, scribes and Pharisees, hypocrites! For you pay tithe of mint and anise and cumin, and have neglected the weightier matters of the law: justice and mercy and faith. These you ought to have done, without leaving the others undone. Blind guides, who strain out a gnat and swallow a camel!"

Matthew 23:23–24 NKJV

No matter what language you're learning, at some point you'll probably come across idioms. How familiar are you with idioms from around the world? "Stop ironing my head!" In Armenian this is said when someone is annoying you. It actually appears in other languages as well – for example, in Turkish, "Don't iron my head!" Here's another one, "Walk around in hot porridge." It is the Czech equivalent of "beat around the bush". The Finnish and Norwegians have also brought cats into the picture, using "Pace around hot porridge like a cat" to mean the same thing. When someone sneezes, usually "Bless you" would suffice, but a more comprehensive version is used by Mongolians, "God bless you and may your moustache grow like brushwood". "To have one's eyes lined with ham" is an Italian idiom when unable to see something that's plainly obvious. In Australia, the idiom "He's got a kangaroo loose in the top paddock" is similar to what we know as "He's got a screw loose". "Riding an elephant to catch a grasshopper" is a Thai idiom applicable when a person puts in a lot of effort to achieve something insignificant.

In today's verse we have a rather unusual phrase. Jesus exclaimed, "Blind guides, who strain out a gnat and swallow a camel!"[493] In this chapter Jesus did not hold back in His indictment of the religious leaders of His day, referring to them as "hypocrites", "blind guides", "brood of

---

[493] Matthew 23:24 NKJV

vipers" and "whitewashed sepulchres". In verse 23, He said, "Woe to you, scribes and Pharisees, hypocrites! For you pay tithe of mint and anise and cumin, and have neglected the weightier matters of the law: justice and mercy and faith. These you ought to have done, without leaving the others undone."[494]

He's saying that they've picked out the smallest matters and obsessed over them, while completely ignoring the core issues, like justice, mercy and faith. To use a common English expression, they "missed the forest for the trees". Jesus followed up in verse 24 with the phrase about straining at a gnat, and swallowing a camel. The Pharisees strained their drinkables with a mesh cloth so that they wouldn't accidentally swallow a gnat, an unclean insect according to the law.[495] Jesus alluded to this practice and then contrasted it with a hyperbolic picture of gulping down a camel. The picture He painted was that of religious leaders squinting at fine gauze to be sure they've captured pinhead-sized impurities, while camels, also unclean animals that were forbidden as food, have been swallowed whole. In this way, Jesus accused them of going to great lengths (straining out gnats) to avoid offence in minor things, while being oblivious to (swallowing camels) of such weightier matters. They were to act with justice and equity toward one another. They were meant to behave with mercy and compassion toward those in need. They were to esteem truth and faithfulness in their dealings with God and their fellow man. Today there are still vestiges of their actions alive and well in all of us. Challenge: In what ways am I straining gnats and swallowing camels in my everyday life? What weightier matters need my attention today?

---

[494] Matthew 23:23 NKJV
[495] Leviticus 11:20–23

70

TO BE EXPERIENCED

"The Israelites called the food manna. It was white like coriander seed, and it tasted like honey wafers."

Exodus 16:31 NLT

Have you noticed how certain phrases are eye-catching? Take a menu by way of example. "Line-caught", "farm-raised", "locally sourced" and "free range" attract attention. Sensory words such as ambrosial, velvety and smooth, even gooey, can cause us to purchase that bar of chocolate. Of course restaurateurs and chocolatiers know the power of persuasion and how to promote their products. I was reading practical tips online (wix.com and Spotify) on how to make your product sell. A key point stressed was that when writing about your product details, talk to your audience directly. Exchange passive texts about the product with direct messages to the customer. An example from wix.com,[496] instead of saying "This organic soap is soft on the hands and smells like a prairie", speak to your customers directly and address their emotions: "Put this organic soap in your main bathroom. Your soft hands will thank you and your house will smell like a prairie." Another useful takeaway was to ask, how does the product make customers feel happier, healthier, or more productive? Refer to the problems, glitches and hassle the product helps to solve.[497] In the words of Shopify, "Don't sell just a product, sell an experience." Also, it was noted that people are often swayed to buy a product with the highest number of positive reviews.

---

[496]https://www.wix.com/blog/ecommerce/2018/10/how-to-write-product-descriptions
[497]   https://www.shopify.co.uk/blog/8211159-9-Simple-Ways-to-write-product-descriptions-that-sell

Today's invitation, Psalm 34:8, comes with many positive reviews and is to be experienced – "Oh, taste and see that the Lord is good! Blessed is the man who takes refuge in him!"[498] The words "taste and see" are addressed directly to you. They are to be experienced.

Imagine you had never seen or tasted a nectarine. You could Google the word "nectarine" and learn about the fruit, its origin, texture, weight, size and other characteristics. You could even become an expert on nectarines by researching them in depth. But imagine if you had never actually tasted one. There is no substitute for actually beholding that sun-kissed globe with a blush of warmth about it, touching its smooth texture (no fuzzy exterior like a suede cushion stroked the wrong way, sorry peaches!), smelling the delectable fragrant aroma exuding from it, biting down into its delicious fruit, savouring the unique flavour dancing over your tongue in swirling crescendo and allowing the overflow of sweet, syrupy juice to trickle down your chin. To experience it is a truly palatable encounter, a celebration on your taste buds.

God wants you to completely experience the delights of who He is. Draw close and discover. Taste of His goodness. Read the reviews of lives transformed by His grace. David intensely yearns for us to experience and enjoy what he has experienced and enjoyed – that's why there's an "Oh …!" at the beginning of his invitation. He is bursting with a passion and desire to bring us into his deep personal experience of God's goodness. God Himself doesn't want us to just read about His goodness or just hear about His goodness but He wants us to fully experience His overflowing goodness in our lives. It is interesting that the first usage of the Hebrew word for "taste" is in Exodus 16:31 in relation to manna, the food from heaven, which God rained down upon the Israelites to show them that He alone was the Lord their God, their source and sufficiency. Every day for forty years in the wilderness, God provided them with this bread from heaven to sustain and nourish them. Israel tasted the goodness of their covenant God daily. God has provided an even greater manna for all those who truly want to taste His goodness: the true Bread from Heaven, Jesus Christ, who brings complete salvation and everlasting life for all those who believe.

---

[498] Psalm 34:7 ESV

71

MADE FOR SHARING

"Then they said to each other, 'What we're doing is not right.
This is a day of good news and we are keeping it to ourselves.'"
2 Kings 7:9 NIV

I have compiled a list of some of the catchiest chocolate related slogans and tag lines. Can you identify which type of chocolate they are the slogans for?

"The lighter way to enjoy chocolate." (Maltesers)

"Feel the bubbles." (Aero)

"A … a day helps you work, rest and play." (Mars)

"The taste of paradise." (Bounty)

"Have a break. Have a …" (KitKat)

"Melts in your mouth, not in your hands." (M&Ms)

"It's not for girls." (Yorkie)

"Full of eastern promise." (Fry's Turkish Delight)

"Do you love anyone enough to give them your last …?" (Rolo)

"It's not Terry's, it's mine." (Chocolate Orange)

"And all because the lady loves …" (Milk Tray)

"They grow on you." (Roses)

"Made for sharing." (Quality Street)

Made for sharing. In 2 Kings 7 we read, "What we're doing is not right. This is a day of good news and we are keeping it to ourselves."[499] Or, "This is not right. This is a day of good news, and we aren't sharing it with anyone!"[500]

At a time of severe famine, four men with leprosy went to the Aramean camp and found that the enemy had fled and there was an

---

[499] 2 Kings 7:9 NIV
[500] 2 Kings 7:9 NLT

abundance of provisions at their disposal. But they realised something of paramount importance. We have good news – we shouldn't keep it to ourselves! They knew that the people in the city could also benefit and be saved. They knew that people who were starving did not need to die. It would have been morally wrong for them be selfish and stay silent. They knew they should not keep such amazing life-saving news to themselves. "This isn't right. We have stumbled upon a good thing, and we have kept it to ourselves."[501]

This is surely a wonderful illustration of our motive for telling others the good news about Jesus Christ. In like manner to these starving men who stumbled upon God's surplus, we have "received grace heaped upon more grace!" [502] As the redeemed of the Lord we have been delivered from the camp of the enemy. This is a day of good news and it's not right that we keep it for ourselves. We have far better news than they had – the good news of Jesus and the Gospel. We have an obligation to God to obey the great commission. And we have an obligation to our neighbours. "And how can they hear, unless someone tells them?"[5035] He has chosen us to be a part of the reaching out process. How beautiful are the feet of those who bring good news. We are the human agents responsible for carrying out God's plans. As someone once quipped, "Every heart without Christ is a mission field, and every heart with Christ is a missionary!"

Thank God for every evidence of His saving grace, for every life transformed, for every broken life healed, for every lost person found, for every one far off brought near. Pray for realisation that we face a task unfinished, that this is a day of good news, that it is not right that we aren't sharing it as we ought. Pray for more courage, more tears, more prayers that avail much, open doors to share Christ and much fruit as a result.

---

[501] 2 Kings 7:9 VOICE
[502] John 1:16 TPT
[503] Romans 10:14 CEV

72

TIMID LIKE TIMOTHY?

"For God has not given us a spirit of timidity, but of power and love and discipline."

2 Timothy 1:7 NASB

*I*n his first letter to Timothy, Paul had urged him not to give way to intimidation. "And don't be intimidated by those who are older than you; simply be the example they need to see by being faithful and true in all that you do. Speak the truth and live a life of purity and authentic love as you remain strong in your faith."[504]

Timothy's courage and zeal had been flagging in the ongoing battle with false teachers and fierce persecution. Paul wrote to him again to address Timothy's tendency toward timidity in the face of persecution and hardship. The Amplified Bible reads, "For God did not give us a spirit of timidity (of cowardice, of craven and cringing and fawning fear), but [He has given us a spirit] of power and of love and of calm and well-balanced mind and discipline and self-control."[505]

The word "timidity" in this verse is translated from the Greek word "deilia", which depicts a cowardly and timid person. First-century historian Josephus used the word to refer to the ten spies who brought back bad reports of the Promised Land and saw themselves as grasshoppers ("We were like grasshoppers in our own sight"[506]). In contrast to them we are told that Caleb had a different spirit.[507]

Challenge: do you have a different spirit or a spirit of timidity? These accounts of old are written for good reason, as Paul said, "These are all

---

[504] 1 Timothy 4:12 TPT
[505] 2 Timothy 1:7 AMPC
[506] Numbers 13:33 NASB
[507] Numbers 14:24

warning markers – danger! – in our history books, written down so that we don't repeat their mistakes. Our positions in the story are parallel – they at the beginning, we at the end – and we are just as capable of messing it up as they were. Don't be so naive and self-confident. You're not exempt. You could fall flat on your face as easily as anyone else. Forget about self-confidence; it's useless. Cultivate God-confidence."[508]

God has not given us a spirit of timidity, but of power and love and discipline. You are empowered. As Paul said, "I have strength for all things in Christ Who empowers me".[509] Or, "I find that the strength of Christ's explosive power infuses me to conquer every difficulty."[510] We are loved and God's love has been poured out into our hearts through the Holy Spirit. John reminds us, "There is no fear in love. But perfect love drives out fear".[511] Another translation states, "Love turns fear out of doors and expels every trace of terror!"[512]

We can have confidence when we comprehend what manner of love the Father has bestowed on us. We have also been given soundness of mind or a disciplined mind, the opposite of a mind given to fear, panic, or unfounded and unreasonable thinking. This word describes a mind that is thinking correctly, governed by the peace of God and guided with godly wisdom.

Receive Paul's words of encouragement. Go ahead, fan into flame the gift of God that is in you. Say farewell to fear. Value the dunamis power and the agape love deposited in you and with soundness of mind know whom you have believed.[513] In Paul's words, "Allow the healing words you've heard from me to live in you and make them a model for life".[514]

---

[508] 1 Corinthians 10:11–12 MSG
[509] Philippians 4:13 AMPC
[510] Philippians 4:13 TPT
[511] 1 John 4:18 NIV
[512] 1 John 4:18 AMPC
[513] 2 Timothy 1:12
[514] 2 Timothy 1:13 TPT

73

CHANGE IS IN THE AIR

"The fragrance of their flowers whispers, 'There is change in the air.' Arise, my love, my beautiful companion, and run with me to the higher place."

Song of Solomon 2:13 TPT

*I*s it going to rain today? Is it going to stay fair? And how can you tell? Evangelista Torricelli, a pupil of Galileo, is the inventor of the barometer, an instrument which measures atmospheric pressure, used especially in forecasting the weather and determining altitude. He made the first barometer, known as the "Torricelli's tube" in Florence, Italy, in 1643. New types of barometers have developed over time, one of which hangs in the hall and gets a tap when passing. The dial reads: stormy – rain – change – fair. A tap can move the hand according to the daily pressure. Changes in the air pressure or barometric pressure mean a change in weather.

The title for today's devotion, "Change is in the Air", is taken from Song of Solomon 2:11–13. Allow the words to minister to you as you read. "The season has changed, the bondage of your barren winter has ended, and the season of hiding is over and gone. The rains have soaked the earth and left it bright with blossoming flowers. The season for singing and pruning the vines has arrived. I hear the cooing of doves in our land, filling the air with songs to awaken you and guide you forth. Can you not discern this new day of destiny breaking forth around you? The early signs of my purposes and plans are bursting forth. The budding vines of new life are now blooming everywhere. The fragrance of their flowers whispers, 'There is change in the air'. Arise, my love, my beautiful companion, and run with me to the higher place."[515]

---

[515] Song of Solomon 2:11–13 TPT

There is change in the air. The barograph indicates transition. The pressure, the bondage of your barren winter has ended. Your season of hiding is over and gone. A new day of destiny bursts forth as Jesus calls you to run into the new level that He has for you. It's a time of fruitfulness and flourishing. There are signs of life all around you! Your life is bursting with Heavenly intention. Can you discern it? Can you not smell it, feel it, touch it and taste it? There is change in the air!

These beautiful personal words call to you and me to run with Him to the higher place. He, Jesus wants your company and wants to lead you out of barrenness into a place of intimacy, growth, vibrancy and a new destiny. Will you go with Him?

A new day of destiny dawns on the people of God corporately. Where things have been desolate and barren, new life is about to spring forth. You can call it awakening, revival, reformation or outpouring, it doesn't really matter, but there is change in the air. The atmosphere is changing. The Father's plans and purposes are about to burst forth!

God says, "Behold, I am doing a new thing! Now it springs forth; do you not perceive and know it and will you not give heed to it? I will even make a way in the wilderness and rivers in the desert."[516]

Nothing can stop the move of the Spirit – nothing can hinder or prevent the mighty outpouring of heaven upon the earth.

---

[516] Isaiah 43:19 AMPC

74

THE TRAIL YOU'RE LEAVING BEHIND

"Then he gave his answer: 'Go back and tell John what you have just seen and heard: The blind see, the lame walk, lepers are cleansed, the deaf hear, the dead are raised, the wretched of the earth have God's salvation hospitality extended to them.'"

Luke 7:21–22 MSG

*L*ook up on a bright sunny day and you might witness white wispy contrails criss-crossing the sky, the by-product of the aviation industry. The term "contrail" is a blend of "condensation trail". Airplanes leave white trails, or contrails, in their wakes for the same reason that we can sometimes see our breath. They form in air above about 25,000 feet, when that air is moist and colder than −40°C. They are basically human-made clouds and researchers are increasingly warning of the thermal blanket they are leaving behind.

Contemporary society is recurrently reminded and cautioned regarding another trail, the trail of data we leave behind. Every day, whether we want to or not, most of us contribute to a growing portrait of who we are online, known as our digital footprint. Your digital footprint can be active or passive. Your active digital footprint is when you take an obvious action such as adding to your Instagram story or posting on Facebook. Your passive digital footprint is built without your express buy-in. If your phone's Bluetooth is on, a nearby takeaway might send you a coupon for lunch. If you open an email sale offer, you leave a passive trail, even if you don't end up buying anything.

Then there's increasing talk about our carbon footprint. It's often stated that the next few years will be decisive in our fight against climate change and success will depend on our ability to reduce our carbon footprint. Every time you travel by car, charge your mobile phone, switch on the television and a host of other gadgetry, you leave a trail of gases in your wake that build up in the atmosphere and contribute to global warming. It is this trace of greenhouse gases produced by us that's known as the carbon footprint.

Today pause and wholeheartedly consider the trail you're leaving behind. As you look back over your life, what do you see? Is there a trail of positive deposits left in people's lives or of negative withdrawals? Is there a trail of being a blessing or of creating havoc? Think for a moment of the contrails of Jesus. When Jesus was asked the question, "Are you the one who is to come, or should we expect someone else?"[517] notice how He answered. "Go back and report to John what you have seen and heard: The blind receive sight, the lame walk, those who have leprosy are cleansed, the deaf hear, the dead are raised, and the good news is proclaimed to the poor."[518]

The trail left behind Jesus was of lives transformed, healed and made whole. As the Bible states, "Jesus went about doing good."[519] Jesus went around doing good to those He met. There was always evidence that Jesus had been in the region. If someone followed you around, would they see a trail of good works? Would they see you going the second mile, turning the other cheek, being the good Samaritan? As disciples of Jesus Christ, we are to follow His example of doing good. We are to place our feet in His footprints, as Peter put it, "He is your example, and you must follow in his steps."[520] The word "follow" is the Greek word "epakoloutheo" meaning to carefully follow after someone with the goal to replicate what he does. The word "steps" is the Greek word "ichnos", a word which really means footprints. Step in His very footprints! Leave a trail of good and grace.

---

[517] Luke 7:21 NIV
[518] Luke 7:22 NIV
[519] Acts 10:38 ESV
[520] 1 Peter 2:21 NLT

75

THE HAND OF GOD

"The Lord's hand was with them, and a great number of people believed and turned to the Lord."

Acts 11:21 NIV

I vaguely remember the stunning moment and furore when Diego Maradona, in the 1986 FIFA World Cup, scored for Argentina against England with an infamous, illegal, but unpenalised handball. Maradona should have received a yellow card for using his hand and the goal disallowed. However, as the referees did not have a clear view of the play and replay technology did not yet exist, the goal stood. The game ended with a 2–1 win for the Argentines, thanks to a second goal scored by Maradona, known as the "Goal of the Century". After the match, Maradona referred to his first goal as "La mano de Dios" or "the hand of God" goal, in later years refuting this by saying what he defined at that time as "la mano de Dios" was "la mano del Diego"!

In the Bible it is encouraging to know that God's mighty hand is steady and sure. Peter tells us, "Therefore humble yourselves under the mighty hand of God, that He may exalt you in due time."[521] We know that God's hand is open and generous, "When you open your generous hand, it's full of blessings, satisfying the longings of every living thing."[522] We are assured that God's hand is strong. "With a strong hand, and with an outstretched arm"[523] He rescued His people. His hand is also dangerous against His enemies, "Your right hand, O Lord, has become glorious in power; Your right hand, O Lord, has dashed the

---

[521] 1 Peter 5:6 NKJV
[522] Psalm 145:16 TPT
[523] Psalm 136:12 NKJV

enemy in pieces."[524] God's righteous hand upholds us, "Fear not, for I am with you; be not dismayed, for I am your God. I will strengthen you, yes, I will help you, I will uphold you with My righteous right hand."[525] Isn't it wonderful to realise that "Even there Your hand shall lead me, and Your right hand shall hold me."[526] His hand empowers His servants, as seen in the example of Elijah. "The hand of the Lord was on Elijah. He girded up his loins and ran before Ahab to the entrance of Jezreel [nearly twenty miles]."[527]

Sometimes God's hand disciplines us, but always for our own good as seen in the life of the Psalmist, "Day and night your hand of discipline was heavy on me. My strength evaporated like water in the summer heat. Finally, I confessed all my sins to you and stopped trying to hide my guilt. I said to myself, 'I will confess my rebellion to the Lord.' And you forgave me! All my guilt is gone."[528]

It's a joy to know that God's hand saves. "Behold, the Lord's hand is not shortened, that it cannot save."[529] The Psalmist urges us, "Sing a new song to the Lord, for he has done wonderful deeds. His right hand has won a mighty victory; his holy arm has shown his saving power!"[530] We see the effects of the hand of God in the book of Acts, "The Lord's hand was with them, and a great number of people believed and turned to the Lord."[531]

Jabez knew the profound significance of the hand of God. He prayed, "'Oh, that You would bless me indeed, and enlarge my territory, that Your hand would be with me, and that You would keep *me* from evil, that I may not cause pain!' So God granted him what he requested."[532] May his prayer be our pattern … that Your hand would be with me … to save, strengthen, discipline, uphold and sustain.

---

[524] Exodus 15:6 NKJV
[525] Isaiah 41:10 NKJV
[526] Psalm 139:10 NKJV
[527] 1 Kings 18:46 AMPC
[528] Psalm 32:4–5 NLT
[529] Isaiah 59:1 NKJV
[530] Psalm 98:1 NLT
[531] Acts 11:21 NIV
[532] 1 Chronicles 4:10 NJKV

76

SET ON HIGH

"The name of the Lord is a strong tower; the righteous run to it and are safe."

Proverbs 18:10 NKJV

God identified His name to Moses as "I Am that I Am", for He is everything that we ever need, in every area of life. One impressive portrayal of the Lord can be seen as a Strong Tower, where the righteous run to Him and are safe. How strong is that tower? David testified, "The Lord is my Rock, my Fortress, and my Deliverer; my God, my keen and firm Strength in Whom I will trust and take refuge, my Shield, and the Horn of my salvation, my High Tower."[533] "My High Tower" or "my place of safety".[534]

During the days when Proverbs was penned, a strong tower was a place of safe refuge, robustly built and heavily fortified. It housed plenteous supplies. It was a site of safety and provision. When an enemy attacked, the people found protection in the strong tower. We read, "When you abide under the shadow of Shaddai, you are hidden in the strength of God Most High. He's the hope that holds me and the stronghold to shelter me, the only God for me, and my great confidence."[535] I love those words, "You are hidden in the strength of God Most High." What a picture of strength! God is indeed a Strong Tower and the righteous run to Him. We are told "and they are safe".[536] Make a note of that word "safe". In Hebrew it is "sagab" with the beautiful meaning of being set aloft, of being inaccessibly high, being set on high and being too high for capture.

---

[533] Psalm 18:2 AMPC
[534] Psalm 18:2 NLT
[535] Psalm 91 :1–2 TPT
[536] Proverbs 18:10 NKJV

I remember, when our children were tiny, how I grasped my cherished china lamp embellished with swans, mantled it in bubble wrap, and reaching for the trap door into the attic said, "I'm just putting this out of harm's way." I knew it would be safe when I set it in that high place, an inaccessible place, far from the patter of little feet. Back in the Psalms David poetically declared, "For in the time of trouble he shall hide me in his pavilion: in the secret of his tabernacle shall he hide me; he shall set me up upon a rock."[537] Or, "He will set me on a rock, high above the fray."[538] Or, "He will place me out of reach on a high rock."[539] The Psalmist prayed, "Be thou my strong habitation, whereunto I may continually resort."[540] You have a strong habitation; the Most High! God says in Psalm 91:14, "Because he has set his love upon Me, therefore I will deliver him; I will set him on high, because he has known My name."[541]

To know His Name is to know His character. Think about the character of God for just a moment. Do you need wonders to be wrought for you? His name is Wonderful; look to Him, the God who works wonders. Do you need counsel and direction? His name is the Counsellor. Run to Him and imbibe His wisdom. Do you need strength and sustaining? He is Mighty God. Draw near to Him and draw from Him. Do you need warmth, embrace, reassurance? He is Everlasting Father, Abba, Father of mercies, Father of compassion. In the shelter of His arms, talk to Him and trust in Him. Do you need peace – external, internal, or eternal? His name is the Prince of Peace, the only One who offers perfect peace. He is the God of all comfort,[542] God of all grace,[543] God of hope.[544] Today, Abba's child, soak in His words from Psalm 62:5–8, "Only God is my Savior, and he will not fail me. For he alone is my safe place. His wraparound presence always protects me as my champion defender. There's no risk of failure with God! So why would I let worry paralyze me, even when troubles multiply around me? … His wraparound presence is all I need, for the Lord is my Savior, my hero, and my life-giving strength. Trust only in God every moment!

---

[537] Psalm 27:5 KJV
[538] Psalm 27:5 VOICE
[539] Psalm 27:5 NLT
[540] Psalm 71:3 KJV
[541] Psalm 91:14 NKJV
[542] 2 Corinthians 1:3 NIV
[543] 2 Peter 5:10 NIV
[544] 2 Peter 5:10 NIV

Tell him all your troubles and pour out your heart-longings to him. Believe me when I tell you – he will help you!"[545]

77

SETTLED

"But may the God of all grace, who called us to His eternal glory by Christ Jesus, after you have suffered a while, perfect, establish, strengthen, and settle you."

1 Peter 5:10 NKJV

Isn't this an amazing verse? It is one of the great benedictions of the Bible. Peter refers to one of God's great names, "the God of all grace". In 2 Corinthians 1:3, God is called "the God of all comfort".[546] "All" carries the idea of comprehensiveness. God's grace is comprehensive for any need of any believer at any time. In the previous chapter, Peter describes the grace of God as "manifold" or multicoloured.[547] God has all kinds of grace for any contingency. The Bible says, "And from the overflow of his fullness we received grace heaped upon more grace!"[548] God has grace sufficient for any situation we may face. Though trials are part and parcel of life, Peter prays for the God of all grace to "perfect, establish, strengthen, and settle you". We are not exempt from suffering, but we are enabled. Let's check out the original intent of these words:

"Perfect" (katartizo) means to mend what has been broken or rent (Barclay's commentary tells us it is a surgical word commonly used for setting a fractured bone); to repair (used of mending fishing nets in Matthew 4:21); to fit out, equip, complete, make one what he ought to be ("May he work perfection into every part of you giving you all that you need to fulfil your destiny"[549]). Peter is saying that God repairs the

---

[546] 2 Corinthians 1:3 NKJV
[547] 1 Peter 4:10 NKJV
[548] John 1:16 TPT
[549] Hebrews 13:21 TPT

damage that sin and suffering have wrought and He makes us what we ought to be, outfitting us for life's journey.

"Establish" (sterizo) means to make stable, render constant. The idea is that we are no longer fluctuating, but fixed. As the Psalmist stated, "My heart is fixed, O God, my heart is fixed."[550] The word is used of Jesus in Luke 9:51 "He steadfastly set His face to go to Jerusalem."[551]

"Strengthen" (sthenoo) means to make strong, to fill with strength, to cause someone to become more able or capable. God strengthens us to meet the demands of life. "He gives power to the weak, and to those who have no might He increases strength."[552]

"Settle" (themelioo) means to lay the foundation, make stable, such as a house upon a rock. The house founded on the rock withstands the storm. To "settle" is to repose upon your foundation. As the hymn says, "My hope is built on nothing less than Jesus' blood and righteousness, I dare not trust the sweetest frame but wholly lean on Jesus' name. On Christ the solid rock I stand. All other ground is sinking sand."[553]

May the God of all grace "perfect, establish, strengthen, and settle you". Linger a little longer on that last word, "settle". God does not want anything to unsettle you. Jesus said, "Peace I leave with you; My [own] peace I now give and bequeath to you. Not as the world gives do I give to you. Do not let your hearts be troubled, neither let them be afraid. [Stop allowing yourselves to be agitated and disturbed; and do not permit yourselves to be fearful and intimidated and cowardly and unsettled.]"[554] He said to Martha, "Martha, my beloved Martha. Why are you upset and troubled, pulled away by all these many distractions?"[555] If you are upset or unsettled, repose afresh upon your foundation. May the God of all grace perfect, establish, strengthen and settle *you*.

---

[550] Psalm 57:7 KJV
[551] Luke 9:51 NKJV
[552] Isaiah 40:29 NKJV
[553] Edward Mote 1834
[554] John 14:27 AMPC
[555] Luke 10:41 TPT

78

WHAT DO YOU SAY ABOUT YOURSELF?

"Finally they said, 'Who are you? Give us an answer to take
back to those who sent us. What do you say about yourself?'"
John 1:22 NIV

*S*omeone quipped, "What do John the Baptist and Winnie-the-Pooh have in common?" Their middle name. We could also say that they both ate honey! Today's verse was addressed to John the Baptist. Unlike most people, John the Baptist's favourite topic of conversation was not himself. When the Jews sent delegates from Jerusalem to investigate and interrogate him, they did not major on discretion as they asked point-blank, "Who are you? Give us an answer to take back to those who sent us. What do you say about yourself?"

John replied, "I am a voice of one calling in the wilderness, 'Make straight the way for the Lord.'"[556]

In other words, if you want to know my job description, read the prophet Isaiah, chapter 40 and verse 3. John's life had a single purpose: to point people to the Messiah. If asked, "Who are you? What do you say about yourself?" how would you answer? Does your conversation bring attention to yourself, or does it point people to Jesus? Think for a moment of how John could have answered the Jewish emissaries. John could have spoken of the supernatural aspect of his birth, how an angel of the Lord called Gabriel predicted his conception to elderly parents Zacharias and Elizabeth, both from the priestly family of Aaron. He could have related how the angel delivered the name God had chosen for him – "You are to call him John."[557] He could have pointed out the fact that he was "filled with the Holy Spirit, even from his mother's womb".[558] He could have detailed how he was "a man sent from God".[559] He could have mentioned how he had amassed a huge

---

[556] John 1:23 NIV
[557] Luke 1:13 NIV
[558] Luke 1:15 ESV
[559] John 1:6 NKJV

following and had his own disciples. Droves of people came to hear him preach and he made an enormous impression on his generation. Had he wanted, he could have even acknowledged that he had a title, "John the Baptist". But instead of drawing attention to himself, he revealed an attitude of humility and always pointed beyond himself to Jesus, "There comes One after me who is mightier than I, whose sandal strap I am not worthy to stoop down and loose."[560] This was a task undertaken by menial servants, yet in John's estimation the Messiah was so much greater that he didn't feel worthy to even loosen His sandal strap.

Surely we need to join John the Baptist in esteeming ourselves less and exalting Christ more. He lived with such a deep sense of commitment to keep Jesus supreme. His motto, "He must become greater; I must become less,"[561] says it all. He had one purpose: to prepare the way for Jesus. He never allowed himself to get sidetracked in building his own kingdom or ensuring that he stayed the centre of attention. We see that he was even content for his disciples to start following Jesus: "Again, the next day, John stood with two of his disciples. And looking at Jesus as He walked, he said, 'Behold the Lamb of God!' The two disciples heard him speak, and they followed Jesus."[562]

The world will always give us opportunities to esteem ourselves more highly than we ought and have an exaggerated opinion of our own importance. Paul stated, "God has given me grace to speak a warning about pride. I would ask each of you to be emptied of self-promotion and not create a false image of your importance."[563] Let's remember that our relevance is always in relation to Jesus.

---

[560] Mark 1:7 NKJV
[561] John 3:30 NIV
[562] John 1:35–37 NKJV
[563] Romans 12:3 TPT

79

HAVE YOU GOT BOTTLE?

"And the Angel of the Lord appeared to him, and said to him, 'The Lord is with you, you mighty man of valor!'"

Judges 6:12 NKJV

"He's got more bottle than a milkman" is an idiomatic way of saying that a person is brave and valiant. Consequently, if someone has lost their bottle, it is implied that they've lost their nerve. They might "bottle out of" something or simply "bottle it" if they do not have the guts to do what they intend.

In the Old Testament we encounter a beautiful Hebrew word, "chayil", which conveys valour, fortitude, guts, mettle, bravery, exceptional or heroic courage when facing danger. Chayil first appears in Joshua 1:14 referring to mighty men of valour, "Your wives, your little ones, and your livestock shall remain in the land which Moses gave you on this side of the Jordan. But you shall pass before your brethren armed, all your mighty men of valor, and help them."[564] Chayil is spelt with three Hebrew letters – Chet, Yod and Lamed. Chet is the picture of a fence, signifying protection, a sanctuary, a place of security. Yod is the picture of the hand or arm and points to a mighty deed. Lamed is the picture of the shepherd's staff and demonstrates the voice of authority or government. Thus, we find in the letters of Chayil that these warriors of Joshua are under strong leadership, performing a mighty work, and providing a place of protection, a sanctuary for their people.

Flip over to Judges and we locate someone threshing wheat in a winepress. The Angel of the Lord appeared to him, and said to him, "The Lord is with you, you mighty man of valor!"[565] The word "valour" is

---

[564] Joshua 1:14 NKJV
[565] Judges 6:12 NKJV

chayil. Gideon may have looked around. Who? Me? He doesn't immediately see himself in this way as is discovered in reading the rest of the chapter. He says, "How can I save Israel? Indeed, my clan is the weakest in Manasseh, and I am the least in my father's house."[566]

Moving further into the writings of Proverbs Solomon asks an intriguing question, "Who can find a virtuous woman? For her price is far above rubies."[567] The word translated as "virtuous" is actually the word "chayil". She is a valiant woman and a mighty warrior. Solomon looks on her as invaluable. Boaz used the same word of Ruth, calling her a woman of chayil in Ruth 3:11: "all my people in the city know that you are a woman of strength (worth, bravery, capability)".[568]

The key to being men and women of chayil is found in Habakkuk 3:19 where we read, "The Lord God is my strength".[569] You guessed it, the word for strength is chayil. The Amplified Bible says, "The Lord God is my Strength, my personal bravery, and my invincible army. He makes my feet like hinds' feet and will make me to walk [not to stand still in terror, but to walk] and make [spiritual] progress upon my high places [of trouble, suffering, or responsibility]!"[570]

The Lord is our source of valour. He is the voice of authority and government in our lives. By His mighty work on the cross He has wrought victory and salvation for us. By His blood He has provided an eternal place of sanctuary for us. If you have placed your trust in Him, He sees you as chayil, mighty men and women of valour. But do you see yourself as a mighty man of valour? Do you see yourself as a virtuous woman? Do you see the Lord God as your Strength?

---

[566] Judges 6:15 NKJV
[567] Proverbs 31:10 KJV
[568] Ruth 3:11 AMPC
[569] Habakkuk 3:19 KJV
[570] Habakkuk 3:19 AMPC

80

TENNIS TERMINOLOGY

"Dear friends, let us continue to love one another, for love comes from God."

1 John 4:7 NLT

ave you ever stopped to ponder the terms of tennis and their origins? "Tennis" itself derives from the French imperative "tenez" which means "hold, take, receive". In the game's medieval beginnings, in twelfth-century France, this word is what players shouted as a fair warning before serving the ball to their opponent. There are many intriguing words used in the game such as let, deuce, serve, volley, advantage, set, umpire, unseeded, not to mention the strange scoring system: 15, 30, 40. Personally, the most baffling of all is the use of the word, "love" used in tennis instead of the word "zero" or "nil". It is used to describe a lack of score in either points, games or sets, i.e., a game score of 40–0 is given as "40 love". Often on a tennis court there seems an absence of love and in the heat of a match tempers flare with combustive exchanges.

So, how did the word "love" wend its way into the game? According to etymologists, the word "love" is possibly derived from the French word "l'oeuf" which literally means egg. If we survey the shape of an egg, we can see that it resembles a zero and thus came to be used when somebody had no score in tennis. Another possible theory, again to do with the word "egg", is that when someone has no score in the sport people have said in the past that they have egg on their face. A further theory is that those with zero points were still playing for the "love of the game" despite their losing score.

Thankfully, the origin of love in the Bible is clear-cut, no ambiguity whatsoever. As John states, "Dear friends, let us continue to love one another, for love comes from God."[571] He also invites us, "Look with wonder at the depth of the Father's marvellous love that he has lavished on us! He has called us and made us his very own beloved children."[572]

God "so loved" us.[573] He demonstrated His own love for us. Paul's desire is for us to discover "the great magnitude of the astonishing love of Christ in all its dimensions. How deeply intimate and far-reaching is his love! How enduring and inclusive it is! Endless love beyond measurement that transcends our understanding – this extravagant love pours into you until you are filled to overflowing with the fullness of God!"[574]

Yes, this love should overflow from us. What does its overflow look like? Paul tells us, "Love is patient; love is kind. Love isn't envious, doesn't boast, brag, or strut about. There's no arrogance in love; it's never rude, crude, or indecent – it's not self-absorbed. Love isn't easily upset. Love doesn't tally wrongs or celebrate injustice; but truth – yes, truth – is love's delight! Love puts up with anything and everything that comes along; it trusts, hopes, and endures no matter what."[575] He points out its varied expressions, "But the fruit produced by the Holy Spirit within you is divine love in all its varied expressions: joy that overflows, peace that subdues, patience that endures, kindness in action, a life full of virtue, faith that prevails, gentleness of heart, and strength of spirit."[576] As we read through the Bible, it is clear that love is never worth nothing. In fact, if you read the words of Paul in 1 Corinthians 13, the word "nothing" applies only if we don't have it.[577]

[571] 1 John 4:7 NLT
[572] 1 John 3:1 TPT
[573] John 3:16 KJV
[574] Ephesians 3:18–19 TPT
[575] 1 Corinthians 13:4–7 VOICE
[576] Galatians 5:22–23 TPT
[577] 1 Corinthians 13:1:2–3 NIV

81

BEARING THAT NAME

"However, if you suffer as a Christian, do not be ashamed, but praise God that you bear that name."

1 Peter 4:16 NIV

Francis Beaufort, Hans Geiger, Jules Léotard, André-Marie Ampère, Rudolf Diesel, the Duke of Wellington, Samuel Morse, Charles Macintosh, Louis Braille and William Henry Hoover all share something in common. They invented or discovered something significant that bears their name. The Beaufort scale, Geiger counter, leotard, ampere, diesel, wellington boots, Morse code, mac, Braille and Hoover are their products which became nouns that bear their name.

We who follow Christ bear His name. Peter tells us, "However, if you suffer as a Christian, do not be ashamed, but praise God that you bear that name."[578] Think deeply of those words, "praise God that you bear that name". Or, "Praise God for the privilege of being called by his name!"[579] The Passion Translation phrases it, "If you suffer for being a Christian, don't consider it a disgrace but a privilege. Glorify God because you carry the Anointed One's name."[580] In Luke's record of the early church he chronicled, "The disciples were first called Christians in Antioch."[581] The church did not call themselves Christian, the people of Antioch did. They were given the appellation because they followed Christ and showed Christlike behaviour. While the term "Christian" was spoken of them with scorn and sarcasm, they embraced it as a badge of honour, a mark of allegiance to Christ. They adopted it as

---

[578] 1 Peter 4:16 NIV
[579] 1 Peter 4:16 NLT
[580] 1 Peter 4:16 TPT
[581] Acts 11:26 NKJV

acknowledgement of the Person and work of Lord Jesus Christ in their lives. As Paul stated, "It is no longer I who live, but Christ lives in me; and the life which I now live in the flesh I live by faith in the Son of God, who loved me and gave Himself for me."[582] Also, "Christ in you, the hope of glory."[583]

Do you recall the commission given to Ananias, how he was told to go to Straight Street, locate Paul and lay his hands on him? Ananias answered, "Lord, I have heard from many about this man, how much harm he has done to Your saints in Jerusalem."[584] Notice the Lord's response, "Go, for he is a chosen vessel of Mine to bear My name before Gentiles, kings, and the children of Israel."[585] Paul was a vessel chosen to bear His name. So are you.

The Bible says, "And whatever you do or say, do it as a representative of the Lord Jesus, giving thanks through him to God the Father."[586] Bearing the name of Jesus carries with it the power of God. Peter, who wrote today's verse, would not have forgotten the time when he and John were walking to the temple at the hour of prayer. On route, they came across a lame man begging for alms. Peter and John looked straight at him and said, "Silver and gold I do not have, but what I do have I give you: In the name of Jesus Christ of Nazareth, rise up and walk."[587] They helped him up and immediately his feet and ankle bones received strength. As this man ran into the temple leaping and praising God, the people were amazed and Peter realised they were looking at him thinking that by his own power or godliness he had made this man walk. Peter quickly pointed them to Jesus. Peter's exact words were, "His name, through faith in His name, has made this man strong."[588] Again, "Let it be known to you all, and to all the people of Israel, that by the name of Jesus Christ of Nazareth, whom you crucified, whom God raised from the dead, by Him this man stands here before you whole."[589] Praise God that we bear His name.

---

[582] Galatians 2:20 NKJV
[583] Colossians 1:27 NKJV
[584] Acts 9:13 NKJV
[585] Acts 9:15 NKJV
[586] Colossians 3:17 NLT
[587] Acts 3:5 NKJV
[588] Acts 3:16 NKJV
[589] Acts 4:10 NKJV

82

THE ROPE OF HOPE

"For I know the plans I have for you," declares the Lord, "plans to prosper you and not to harm you, plans to give you hope and a future."

Jeremiah 29:11 NIV

There is a beautiful Hebrew word tucked into the folds of Scripture, well worth unfurling. The Bible tells us, "The unfolding of your words gives light; it gives understanding to the simple."[590] We pray that as we dwell on the word "tikvah" today, we will receive understanding of its true intent. It is the Hebrew word for hope, found in the well-known words, "'For I know what I have planned for you,' says the Lord. 'I have plans to prosper you, not to harm you. I have plans to give you a future filled with hope.'"[591] The Psalmist chose the word, "For You are my hope, O Lord God; You are my trust from my youth"[592] and "I wait for the Lord, my soul waits, and in His word I do hope."[593] "Hatikvah", "The Hope", is Israel's national anthem. *Strong's Concordance* defines "Tikvah" as a cord, expectation and hope. Its first occurrence in the Bible is in Joshua 2, the account of the two Israelite spies and the woman Rahab of Jericho. Having hidden the men and helped them escape they said to her, "This oath you made us swear will not be binding on us unless, when we enter the land, you have tied this scarlet cord in the window through which you let us down, and unless you have brought your father and mother, your brothers and all your family into your house."[594] We read, "So she

---

[590] Psalm 119:130 NIV
[591] Jeremiah 29:11 NET
[592] Psalm 71:5 NKJV
[593] Psalm 130:5 NKJV
[594] Joshua 2:17–18 NIV

sent them away, and they departed. And she tied the scarlet cord in the window."[595] While "tikvah" is used here in its literal sense as a "cord or rope" it also reveals the figurative picture of hope. It was the cord that gave her hope, her lifeline. It was her only assurance that her household would be spared by the Israelites. It was emblematic of her faith.

Hebrews 11, a chapter of faith where Rahab is mentioned as an example, begins with the words, "Now faith is the substance of things hoped for".[596] Did you note that Rahab's cord was a scarlet cord? Surely this is symbolic of the blood of the Lamb at Passover, reminding us that our hope is in our Passover Lamb, Jesus Christ. We know from reading ahead that Rahab's family were saved as promised; she went on to marry Salmon and as such became the great-great-grandmother of King David.[597] Thus, she was key in the lineage of Jesus.

As Paul writes his first letter to Timothy, his opening words remind us of "Christ Jesus, who is our hope."[598] To Titus he writes, "We wait for the blessed hope – the appearing of the glory of our great God and Savior, Jesus Christ."[599] Peter spoke of "a living hope through the resurrection of Jesus Christ from the dead."[600] Jesus not only came to bring hope. He is our hope. Remember that at one time we were hopeless. As the Bible put it, "You were without Christ, being aliens from the commonwealth of Israel and strangers from the covenants of promise, having no hope and without God in the world. But now in Christ Jesus you who once were far off have been brought near by the blood of Christ."[601] He is your scarlet cord, "Christ in you, the hope of glory."[602] He has plans to give you a future filled with hope.

---

[595] Joshua 2:21 NIV
[596] Hebrews 11:1 NKJV
[597] Matthew 1:5
[598] 1 Timothy 1:1 NASB
[599] Titus 2:13 NIV
[600] 1 Peter 1:3 NIV
[601] Ephesians 2:12–13 NKJV
[602] Colossians 1:27 NKJV

83

FAREWELL

"The grace of the Lord Jesus Christ, and the love of God, and the communion of the Holy Spirit be with you all. Amen."

2 Corinthians 13:14 NKJV

*V*alediction, according to the dictionary, is the act of bidding farewell.[603] Originating in Latin roots which mean "to say goodbye" it is the greeting counterpart to salutation. We have many expressions for saying farewell such as those given to us by the Von Trapp children in *The Sound of Music*, "So long, farewell, auf Wiedersehen, goodbye".[604] Curiosity prompted me to delve into the etymology of these words. "So long" is from the Irish for goodbye (slán), meaning "safe/favourable", conveying the sense of having a favourable and safe journey. Its intent reminds me of 3 John 2, "Beloved, I pray that you may prosper in all things and be in health, just as your soul prospers."[605] The Greek word for "prosper" is a combination of two words, "eu" meaning "good" and "hodos" meaning "path/journey" and thus conveys the idea of having a good and safe journey. May it go well with you. May you prosper. So long. Akin is the word "farewell", a combination of "fare" and "well". The old word "fare" meant "journey", hence the expression wishes someone a favourable journey.

How about the word "goodbye"? It's an Old English contraction of the phrase "God be with you (or ye)". That was its original intent. What a beautiful parting phrase. Today, saying "bye" has the same basic meaning as "goodbye" but we've completely lost the original meaning

---

[603] https://www.merriam-webster.com
[604] Song from Rodgers and Hammerstein's 1959 musical, *The Sound of Music*
[605] 3 John 2 NKJV

of the phrase. Really, we're just saying "be with ye" which doesn't really make any sense. God be with you.

At the conclusion of 2 Corinthians 13:14 we locate a lovely farewell greeting of Paul, "The grace of the Lord Jesus Christ, and the love of God, and the communion of the Holy Spirit be with you all. Amen."[606] Paul wanted the Corinthian Christians to be completely blessed by everything God is. We call this verse a benediction. Our God is our great Benefactor whose goodness we taste and see on a daily basis. Because of His generous grace, lavish love and constant communion we lack no beneficial thing.

Paul knew of God's grace firsthand: "The grace of our Lord was poured out on me abundantly, along with the faith and love that are in Christ Jesus."[607] Having been saved by grace, he then lived by grace, dedicating his life "to testify to the gospel of the grace of God".[608] He also knew of God's love firsthand, speaking of how "God demonstrates his own love for us in this: while we were still sinners, Christ died for us."[609] Paul wanted us to put on God's love, to be rooted and established in love and to experience its vast dimensions. Paul also knew the communion of the Holy Spirit. He wrote of how "the Spirit helps us in our weakness. For we do not know what to pray for as we ought, but the Spirit himself intercedes for us with groanings too deep for words".[610] He personally knew the leading of the Holy Spirit and testified, "My message and my preaching were not with wise and persuasive words, but with a demonstration of the Spirit's power."[611] He prayed, "that He would grant you, according to the riches of His glory, to be strengthened with might through His Spirit in the inner man".[612]

"The amazing grace of the Master, Jesus Christ, the extravagant love of God, the intimate friendship of the Holy Spirit, be with all of you."[613]

---

[606] 2 Corinthians 13:14 NKJV
[607] 1 Timothy 1:14 NIV
[608] Acts 20:24 NKJV
[609] Romans 5:8 NIV
[610] Romans 8:26 ESV
[611] 1 Corinthians 2:4 NIV
[612] Ephesians 3:16 NKJV
[613] 1 Corinthians 13:14 MSG

84

THE WORD OF CHRIST

"Let the word of Christ dwell in you richly"

Colossians 3:16 NKJV

"Let the word of Christ dwell in you richly". Such a rich indwelling will greatly enrich your entire life. Another translation reads, "Let the word of the Anointed One richly inhabit your lives."[614] "The Word that God speaks is alive and full of power." [615] It is vital and vitalising. It enlightens and enriches. It revives the soul, makes wise the simple, brings joy to the heart and gives insight for living.[616] It makes us wise to salvation. It's our training in righteousness. It enables us to be "complete and proficient, well-fitted and thoroughly equipped for every good work".[617]

Jesus said, "If you abide in Me, and My words abide in you, you will ask what you desire, and it shall be done for you."[618] He told us, "It is the Spirit who gives life; the flesh profits nothing. The words that I speak to you are spirit, and they are life."[619] His words are "spirit and life". They quicken the spirit and impart eternal life. That's why Peter says five verses later, "Lord, to whom shall we go? You have the words of eternal life."[620]

"Let the word of Christ dwell in you richly". This surely implies that we need to hear it, heed it, hide it in our hearts, handle it correctly and hold it firmly.

---

[614] Colossians 3:16 VOICE
[615] Hebrews 4:12 AMPC
[616] Psalm 19:7–8
[617] 2 Timothy 3:17 AMPC
[618] John 15:7 NKJV
[619] John 6:63 NKJV
[620] John 6:68 NKJV

Hear it – God said to Ezekiel, "Son of man, listen carefully and take to heart all the words I speak to you."[621] These words apply to us as well, *listen carefully and take to heart all the words I speak to you.* Jesus stated, "Therefore everyone who hears these words of mine and puts them into practice is like a wise man who built his house on the rock."[622] Paul affirmed, "So faith comes from hearing, and hearing by the word of Christ."[623]

Heed it – The Psalmist poses a question and then answers the question himself, "How can a young man cleanse his way? By taking heed according to Your word."[624] The purpose of our hearing it is so that we heed it. Or as Joshua 1:8 tells us, "You shall meditate on it day and night, that you may observe to do according to all that is written in it."[625] Observe to do. Jesus pronounced, "You are My friends if you do whatever I command you."[626] James gave us the timely reminder, "But be doers of the word, and not hearers only, deceiving yourselves."[627]

Hide it – "Thy Word have I hid in my heart that I might not sin against Thee."[628] We internalise the word through meditating on it day and night. Joshua was told that when he did so, then "you shall make your way prosperous, and then you shall deal wisely and have good success."[629] Meditate! Ruminate! Saturate your spirit! Let His words drench you like the refreshing waters of a cool mountain stream. Let them shape how you think and live.

Handle it correctly – One of the last things Paul told Timothy was, "Do your best to present yourself to God as one approved, a worker who does not need to be ashamed and who correctly handles the word of truth."[630] To correctly handle the word of truth we need insight and understanding from the Holy Spirit. Jesus said that the Holy Spirit "will

---

[621] Ezekiel 3:10 NIV
[622] Matthew 7:24 NIV
[623] Romans 10:17 NASB
[624] Psalm 119:9 NKJV
[625] Joshua 1:8 NKJV
[626] John 15:14 NKJV
[627] James 1:22 NKJV
[628] Psalm 119:11 KJV
[629] Joshua 1:8 AMPC
[630] 2 Timothy 2:15 NIV

teach you all things and will remind you of everything I have said to you."[631]

Hold firmly to the word of life – Paul motivated us to "hold firmly to the word of life".[632] Hold your position in it. Stay with the word of life; don't sway with every word of teaching. Let the word of Christ dwell in you richly. Then you will have the mind of Christ and hold the thoughts, feelings and purposes of His heart.

---

[631] John 14:26 NIV
[632] Philippians 2:16 NIV

85

NAAMAN, OR YOUR NAME?

"if the prophet had told you to do something great, would you not have done it? How much more then, when he says to you, 'Wash, and be clean'?"

2 Kings 5:13 NKJV

*J*esus says of Naaman, "And there were many in Israel with leprosy in the time of Elisha the prophet, yet not one of them was cleansed – only Naaman the Syrian."[633] 2 Kings 5 gives us the nitty-gritty of his narrative. As we review his case, let's ask ourselves, instead of Naaman, could it be our name? Naaman needed healing; we need salvation, wholeness in spirit, soul and body.

First, he thought he could buy the cure. He started out "carrying as gifts 750 pounds of silver and 150 pounds of gold."[634] The purchase of indulgences, the mendacity of merit and earning salvation have robbed people of finding the joy of salvation. The Bible invites us, "Come, everyone who thirsts, come to the waters; and he who has no money, come, buy and eat! Come, buy wine and milk without money and without price."[635] Salvation is on the ground of pure, sovereign grace. Salvation is not for sale. Rather we are bought with the precious blood of Christ. In Peter's words, "For you know that it was not with perishable things such as silver or gold that you were redeemed from the empty way of life handed down to you from your ancestors, but with the precious blood of Christ, a lamb without blemish or defect."[636] It is a gift from God. "God saved you by His grace when you believed. And you can't take credit for this; it is a gift from God. Salvation is not a

---

[633] Luke 4:27 NIV
[634] 2 Kings 5:5 NLT
[635] Isaiah 55:1, ESV
[636] 1 Peter 1:18–19 NIV

reward for the good things we have done, so none of us can boast about it."[637]

Naaman also went to the wrong place to be cured. The Jewish maid in Naaman's home told her mistress that there was a "prophet" in Israel who could heal Naaman of his leprosy. He went to the king instead of to Elisha.[638] Many today are knocking at the wrong door for salvation. There is only one door, "I am the door."[639] There is only one way, "I am the way … No one can come to the Father except through me."[640] There is only one name, "Salvation is found in no one else, for there is no other name under heaven given to mankind by which we must be saved."[641]

Notice as well that Naaman wanted to be cured in his own way. Naaman had a fixed opinion as to how it should happen. God's way was outlined in verse 10, and verses 11–12 tell us of Naaman's reaction when he learned of God's method of cleansing. With derision he exclaims, "'Are not Abana and Pharpar, the rivers of Damascus, better than all the waters of Israel? Couldn't I wash in them and be cleansed?' So he turned and went off in a rage."[642] Another translation reads, "He stomped off, mad as a hornet."[643] He does not even condescend to call the Jordan a river. God's way is simple and effective. Call (Romans 10:13); come (Matthew 11:28); enter (John 10:9); receive (John 1:12).

Finally, don't miss this, "Now I know that there is no God in all the world except in Israel."[644] Naaman was now absolutely convinced and determined to make God his God, to know Him, to love Him, to serve Him and to make Him known to others! Just a little previously he had proudly and wrathfully said, "Behold, I thought".[645] Now he gratefully exclaims, "Now I know." Can you say the same?

---

[637] Ephesians 2:8–9 NLT
[638] 2 Kings 5:6
[639] John 10:9 NKJV
[640] John 14:6 NKJV
[641] Acts 4:12 NIV
[642] 2 Kings 5:12 NIV
[643] 2 Kings 5:12 MSG
[644] 2 Kings5:15 NIV
[645] 2Kings 5:11 NIV

86

IN THE KNOW

"Yes, furthermore, I count everything as loss compared to the possession of the priceless privilege (the overwhelming preciousness, the surpassing worth, and supreme advantage) of knowing Christ Jesus my Lord and of progressively becoming more deeply and intimately acquainted with Him [of perceiving and recognizing and understanding Him more fully and clearly]."

Philippians 3:8 AMPC

Philippians 3:8, today's verse, is quite the statement. French commentator Bonnard calls verses 4–7 "one of the most remarkable personal confessions which antiquity has bequeathed to us".[646] You are hearing the distillation of Paul's deepest deliberations. Paul follows it with the words, "I want to know Christ."[647] Or, "that I may know Him".[648] Or, "[For my determined purpose is] that I may know Him [that I may progressively become more deeply and intimately acquainted with Him, perceiving and recognizing and understanding the wonders of His Person more strongly and more clearly]."[649] This knowledge is not esoteric enlightenment such as the mystic philosophers spoke about, but a growing personal relationship. In John 14:8–9 Philip, after following Jesus for a number of years, said to Him, "Lord, show us the Father, and it is sufficient for us." Jesus said to him, "Have I been with you so long, and yet you have not known Me, Philip?"[650]

---

[646] P. Bonnard, *L'Epître de Saint Paul aux Philippiens* (Commentaire du Nouveau Testament, 1950), cited in Martin 144.

[647] Philippians 3:10 NIV

[648] Philippians 3:10 NKJV

[649] Philippians 3:10 AMPC

[650] John 14:8–9 NKJV

Paul not only wanted to know Christ more deeply and intimately himself, he prayed for us to be in the know. In Ephesians 1 he prays, "that the God of our Lord Jesus Christ, the Father of glory, may give to you the spirit of wisdom and revelation in the knowledge of Him, the eyes of your understanding being enlightened; that you may know what is the hope of His calling".[651] Ephesians 3: "[You] may be able to comprehend with all the saints what is the width and length and depth and height – to know the love of Christ which passes knowledge; that you may be filled with all the fullness of God."[652] Peter wanted us to "grow in the grace and knowledge of our Lord and Savior Jesus Christ".[653]

Do you know about His grace? "For you know the grace of our Lord Jesus Christ, that though He was rich, yet for your sakes He became poor, that you through His poverty might become rich."[654] Do you know He whom you believed? "I know whom I have believed and am persuaded that He is able to keep what I have committed to Him until that Day."[655] Do you know the price of your redemption? "For you know that it was not with perishable things such as silver or gold that you were redeemed from the empty way of life handed down to you from your ancestors, but with the precious blood of Christ, a lamb without blemish or defect."[656] Do you know He is in control? "And we know that all things work together for good to those who love God, to those who are the called according to His purpose."[657] Do you know that your work for Him is not pointless? "Therefore, my beloved brethren, be steadfast, immovable, always abounding in the work of the Lord, knowing that your labor is not in vain in the Lord."[658]

[651] Ephesians 1:16–18 NKJV
[652] Ephesians 3:18–19 NKJV
[653] 2 Peter 3:18 NKJV
[654] Ephesians 2:9 NKJV
[655] 2 Timothy 1:12 NKJV
[656] 1 Peter 1:18–19 NIV
[657] Romans 8:28 NKJV
[658] 1 Corinthians 15:58 NKJV

87

SHINING FACES

"The Lord bless you, and keep you [protect you, sustain you, and guard you]; the Lord make His face shine upon you [with favor]"
Numbers 6:24–25 AMP

It wasn't too long ago that our only facial care options were day cream and night cream. Browse the range today and you can acquire ultra-rich regenerist cream, luminous whip, anti-aging, lift and luminate, glow enhancer, refortifying, recushioning, reactivating radiance cream, to name a few examples. Notice the emphasis is on glow, radiance and lumination.

In descending from Sinai with the tablets in hand, "Moses did not know that the skin of his face shone because he had been talking with God … behold, the skin of his face shone."[659] Edmond Locard, known as the Sherlock Holmes of France, formulated the basic principle of forensic science which states, "Every contact leaves a trace." The light on the face of Moses was the result of his contact and fellowship with God. Moses had been in God's presence and his face shone as a result. It is hard to imagine luminescent skin but the Hebrew word has the idea of sending out rays, emitting beams, radiating. David, speaking of God, tells us, "Those who look to him are radiant, and their faces shall never be ashamed."[660] Or, "Gaze upon him, join your life with his, and joy will come. Your faces will glisten with glory. You'll never wear that shame-face again."[661]

Do you consider yourself to be radiant? If not, what has diminished your light?

---

[659] Exodus 34:29–30 ESV
[660] Psalm 34: 5 ESV
[661] Psalm 34:5 TPT

In the New Testament we read of Stephen, the first Christian martyr, "At this point everyone in the high council stared at Stephen, because his face became as bright as an angel's."[662] Covered with a supernatural lustre, Stephen's persecutors looked intently at him.

Consider also the face of Jesus. Matthew tells us, "As the men watched, Jesus' appearance was transformed so that his face shone like the sun, and his clothes became as white as light."[663] Peter, one of the three disciples who witnessed this, wrote, "We were eyewitnesses of his majesty."[664] When John saw Jesus in his vision many years later, "his face was like the sun shining in full strength".[665]

The Psalmist prayed, "May God be gracious to us and bless us and make his face to shine upon us, Selah."[666] "Make your face shine down upon us"[667] and "Make your face shine on your servant."[668] Such words echo the Aaronic blessing in Numbers 6, "The Lord bless you and keep you; the Lord make his face shine on you and be gracious to you; the Lord turn his face toward you and give you peace."[669] The Amplified Bible reads, "The Lord bless you, and keep you [protect you, sustain you, and guard you]; the Lord make His face shine upon you [with favor], and be gracious to you [surrounding you with lovingkindness]; the Lord lift up His countenance (face) upon you [with divine approval], and give you peace [a tranquil heart and life]."

May God's radiance radiate in the habitat of our lives giving glory back to Him.

---

[662] Acts 6:15 NLT

[663] Matthew 17:2 NLT

[664] 2 Peter 1:16 NIV

[665] Revelation 1:16 ESV

[666] Psalm 67:1 ESV

[667] Psalm 80:3,7,19 NLT

[668] Psalm 119:135 NKJV

[669] Numbers 6:24–26 NIV

88

LEAVE YOUR WATER POT

"but whoever drinks the water I give them will never thirst."
John 4:14 NIV

She is never named, yet her encounter with Jesus gives us the longest recorded conversation between the Messiah and any other individual in the Gospel of John. A female in a society where women are both disparaged and disregarded, a race traditionally disdained by Jews, and living in shame as a societal pariah, she not only has a holy encounter with Jesus Christ but also receives the gift of salvation. And her testimony convinces an entire town to believe too.

Decades of decadent living had taken its toll. Her past was tattooed with emotional scars of broken relationships. Her present was tabooed as she lived with one not her husband. Her presence was avoided as we note that she went to the well alone. Why else would she have gone when the sun was at its peak, while other women typically drew water in groups in the morning in a social setting? Nonetheless her heart was wooed by the words of a loving Messiah. "If you knew the Gift of God".[670] If you knew the Wonderful Counsellor … If you knew the Good Shepherd … If you knew the Atoning Sacrifice for your sins … If you knew the Balm of Gilead who soothes your hurts … If you knew the Christ, the Messiah … If you knew the friend of sinners … If you knew the Fountain of living waters … If you knew the Great High Priest who is touched with the feeling of your infirmities … If you knew Jesus, the Saviour … If you knew the Lifter of your head … If you knew the Prince of peace … If you knew the Sun of righteousness with healing in his wings … If you knew the Way, the truth and the life … If you knew the Name above all names. "If you knew the Gift of God", the indescribable gift.

Jesus said, "If you knew the gift of God and who it is that asks you for a drink, you would have asked him and he would have given you

---

[670] John 4:10 NIV

living water."[671] This meeting was no random encounter. Jesus chose to pass through the town of Samaria, a place that many Jews skirted. There was no such animosity in the heart of Jesus, and a Divine orchestration was the occasion of His taking the direct road. The Bible tells us, "Now he had to go through Samaria. So he came to a town in Samaria called Sychar".[672] The name "Sychar" meaning "drunken" seems to have been a term of reproach intimating that it was the seat of drunkards. What a fitting setting for Jesus to offer life-giving water! Jesus told the woman at the well, "Everyone who drinks this water will be thirsty again, but whoever drinks the water I give them will never thirst. Indeed, the water I give them will become in them a spring of water welling up to eternal life."[673] She had drunk from many broken cisterns that could not hold water but now she met the Fountain of living water. The Samaritan woman came to the well with an empty waterpot and an empty heart. But, leaving her waterpot behind, she went away full, with rivers of living water flowing from within and a testimony that transformed an entire community. We read, "Many of the Samaritans from that town believed in him because of the woman's testimony … They said to the woman, 'We no longer believe just because of what you said; now we have heard for ourselves, and we know that this man really is the Savior of the world.'."[674]

Go to the well today. Jesus is already there, ready to talk. He says to you, "I who speak to you am He."[675] Jesus is more than just a story on a page. So, lay down your waterpot, let Him fill you and meet your deepest heart needs.

---

[671] John 4:10 NIV
[672] John 4:4–5 NIV
[673] John 4:13 NIV
[674] John 4:39, 42 NIV
[675] John 4:26 NIV

89

HOW!

"Lord, our Lord, how majestic is your name in all the earth!"

Psalm 8:1 NIV

"Bang", "screamer", "ecphoneme", "shriek", "pling", "the punctus admirativus", "note of admiration": the exclamation mark has gone by many appellations. One theory of its origin posits its derivation from a superimposing of the I and O of the Latin exclamation "Io!" which translates to "joy". Since all letters were written as capitals, an I with an o below it looked a lot like an exclamation point. Over time the "I" stretched out and the dot shrunk to what we know it today. It is essentially shorthand for joy. Although the exclamation mark has enabled expression of strong emotion on paper since the fifteenth century, this upstanding punctuation mark didn't acquire its own dedicated typewriter key until the 1970s. Women apparently outdo men in the use of exclamation marks. Unbelievable, right?! Scripture gives us some exclamatory sentences of how amazing God really is.

How majestic is Your Name in all the earth! "Lord, our Lord, how majestic is your name in all the earth!"[676] "Name" refers to God's essence and character. God is majestic. He is "robed in majesty".[677] David praised God saying, "Yours, O Lord, is the greatness, the power and the glory, the victory and the majesty; for all that is in heaven and in earth is Yours; Yours is the kingdom, O Lord, and You are exalted as head over all"[678] and "I will meditate on the glorious splendor of Your majesty".[679]

---

[676] Psalm 8:1 NIV
[677] Psalm 93:1 NIV
[678] 1 Chronicles 29:11 NKJV
[679] Psalm 145:5 NKJV

How great is Your Goodness! "Oh, how great is Your goodness, which You have laid up for those who fear, revere, and worship You, goodness which You have wrought for those who trust and take refuge in You before the sons of men!"[680] We are encouraged to give thanks to the Lord, for He is good! No good thing does He withhold from us. His goodness and mercy follow us all our days.

How priceless is Your unfailing love! "How priceless is your unfailing love, O God! People take refuge in the shadow of your wings. They feast on the abundance of your house; you give them drink from your river of delights."[681] God's love is constant, consistent and steadfast. He so loves. Greater love has no one than His and nothing can separate us from His love.

How sweet are Your words! "How sweet are your words to my taste, sweeter than honey to my mouth!"[682] We fall in love with God's Word when we fall in love with the Author Himself. His words are sweeter than honey because everything that comes from Him is edifying. When the prophet Ezekiel ate the scroll of the Word of God he remarked, "So I ate, and it was in my mouth like honey in sweetness."[683]

How awesome are Your deeds! "Say to God, 'How awesome are your deeds!'."[684] Something awesome inspires awe. Nowadays the word awesome has been watered down through overuse. We need to discern its distinctiveness. He is "the great and awesome God".[685] How majestic is Your Name in all the earth! How great is Your Goodness! How priceless is Your unfailing love! How sweet are Your words! How awesome are Your deeds!

---

680 Psalm 31:19 AMPC
681 Psalm 36:7–8 NIV
682 Psalm 119:103 NIV
683 Ezekiel 3:3 NKJV
684 Psalm 66:3 NIV
685 Nehemiah 1:5 NIV

90

GARMENTS OF GRACE

"Rather, clothe yourselves with the Lord Jesus Christ, and do not think about how to gratify the desires of the flesh."

Romans 13:14 NIV

The Northern Ireland forecast as I write states, "It will be cloudy during the morning with outbreaks of rain, soon turning showery. Some drier spells in the afternoon with skies brightening at times. It will feel cool or rather cold in the fresh to strong northerly winds. Maximum temperature 12°C. Outlook: Cloudy with showers or longer outbreaks of rain."[686] One thing I have learned over the years is not to be stopped by inclement weather. Simply don outdoor apparel, bundle up and go for it. As fell-walker Alfred Wainwright is popularly attributed as saying, "There's no such thing as bad weather, only unsuitable clothing."

Colossians 3 reminds us that God has a wardrobe picked out for us, suitable clothing for whatever we need to weather. "Therefore, as God's chosen people, holy and dearly loved, clothe yourselves with compassion, kindness, humility, gentleness and patience. Bear with each other and forgive one another if any of you has a grievance against someone. Forgive as the Lord forgave you. And over all these virtues put on love, which binds them all together in perfect unity."[687]

You are already God's chosen one, God's holy one, God's loved one. What an expression of value assigned in Christ. Now He says, put on the character that reflects your new identity. You are to actively clothe yourself with characteristics that mark the believer. You are to be mantled with compassion, accessorised with kindness, humility, gentleness and patience, clothed in forgiveness and the all-purpose

---

[686] metoffice.gov.uk
[687] Colossians 3:12–14 NIV

garment of love. Isn't Jesus all of these things? You are clothing yourself with Christ's attributes. The Message Bible puts it, "So, chosen by God for this new life of love, dress in the wardrobe God picked out for you: compassion, kindness, humility, quiet strength, discipline. Be even-tempered, content with second place, quick to forgive an offense. Forgive as quickly and completely as the Master forgave you. And regardless of what else you put on, wear love. It's your basic, all-purpose garment. Never be without it."[688]

When I'm channel surfing (on TV) and land on a football match, I know which teams are playing because of what they are wearing. I immediately identify them because of their appearance (unless they are wearing their away kit or third kit). Our identity in Christ means we should look, sound, think and behave in a Christlike manner. We should be identified by our kit as outlined earlier. Take a moment to look over and pray over that list. Does it describe you? Is it time for some wardrobe adjustment? What are you wearing? Consider each piece of clothing. Compassion. Kindness. Humility. Gentleness. Patience. Forgiveness. Love. Define and understand what each one represents. Paul tells us in Romans, "Clothe yourselves with the Lord Jesus Christ."[689] "Clothe yourselves" can be translated "put on" or "envelop in". Our clothes, or grace garments, reflect our calling and never go out of style. Go ahead – dress in the wardrobe God Himself picked out for you.

---

[688] Colossians 3:12–14 MSG
[689] Romans 13:14 NIV

Printed in Great Britain
by Amazon

60478680R00109